for 3 - 9s

Book 2

CHRISTIAN FOCUS PUBLICATIONS

We believe that the Bible is God's word to mankind, and that it contains everything we need to know in order to be reconciled with God and live in a way that is pleasing to him. Therefore, we believe it is vital to teach children accurately from the Bible, being careful to teach each passage's true meaning in an appropriate way for children, rather than selecting a 'children's message' from a Biblical passage.

© TnT Ministries
29 Buxton Gardens, Acton, London, W3 9LE
Tel: (0181) 992 0450

Published in 1997 by Christian Focus Publications Ltd.
Geanies House, Fearn, Tain, Ross-shire, IV20 1TW
Tel: (01862) 871 011 Fax: (01862) 871 699

Reprinted 2000

Cover design by Douglas McConnach

This book and others in the series can be purchased from your local Christian bookshop. Alternatively you can write to TnT Ministries direct or place your order with the publisher.

ISBN 1-85792-319-7

TnT Ministries (which stands for Teaching and Training) was launched in February 1993 by Christians from a broad variety of denominational backgrounds who are concerned that teaching the Bible to children be taken seriously. They have been in charge of the Sunday School of 50 teachers at St Helen's Bishopsgate, an evangelical church in the City of London, for 13 years, during which time a range of Biblical teaching materials has been developed. TnT Ministries also runs training days for Sunday School teachers.

Printed in Great Britain by J W Arrowsmith Ltd, Bristol

CONTENTS

On the Way for 3-9s / Book 2

Preparation of Bible material:
Thalia Blundell
David & Christine James

Editing:
David Jackman

Illustrations:
Ben Desmond

Craft Activities:
Thalia Blundell
Trevor Blundell
Hazel Bristow
Julie Farrell
Annie Gemmill
Debbie Levett

On the Way works on a three year syllabus. It covers the main Bible stories from Genesis to the Acts of the Apostles. All the Bible stories are taught as truth and not myth.

Each year the birth of Jesus is taught at Christmas, and the death and resurrection of Jesus at Easter. Between Christmas and Easter the syllabus covers aspects of Jesus' life and teaching, and after Easter there is a short series on the Early Church. The rest of the year is spent looking at the Old Testament stories, covering broad sweeps of Old Testament history. In this way leaders and children gain an orderly and cohesive view of God's dealings with his people throughout the Old and New Testaments.

The lessons are grouped in series, each of which is introduced by a series overview stating the aims of the series, the lesson aim for each week and an appropriate memory verse.

Every lesson, in addition to a lesson aim, has Bible study notes to enable the teacher to understand the passage, suggestions for visual aids and an activity for the children to take home. One activity is suitable for 3-5 year olds, one for 5-7 year olds and one for 7-9s.

How to Prepare a Lesson

To prepare a Sunday School lesson properly takes at least one evening (2-3 hours). It is helpful to read the Bible passage several days before teaching it to allow time to mull over what it is saying.

When preparing a lesson the following steps should be taken -

1. PRAY!

In a busy world this is very easy to forget. We are unable to understand God's word without his help and we need to remind ourselves of that fact before we start.

2. READ THE BIBLE PASSAGE

This should be done **before** reading the lesson manual. Our resource is the Bible, not what someone says about it. The Bible study notes in the lesson manual are a commentary on the passage to help you understand it.

3. LOOK AT THE LESSON AIM

This should reflect the main teaching of the passage. Plan how that can be packaged appropriately for the age group you teach.

4. STORYTELLING

Decide how to tell the Bible story. Is it appropriate to recapitulate on what has happened in previous weeks? Will you involve the children in the presentation of the story? What sort of questions are appropriate to use? How will you ascertain what has been understood? Is there anything in the story that should be applied to their lives?

5. VISUAL AIDS

What type of visual aid will help bring the story alive for the children? Simple pictures may be appropriate. For stories with a lot of movement it may be better to use flannelgraphs or suedegraphs. In some instances models may be appropriate, e.g. the paralysed man being let down through a hole in the roof. Do remember that visual aids take time to make and this will need to be built into your lesson preparation.

6. CRAFT ACTIVITIES

Many of the craft activities require prior preparation by the teacher so do not leave it until the night before!

Benefits of On The Way

- Encourages the leaders to study the Bible for themselves.
- Chronological approach gives leaders and children a proper view of God's dealings with his people.
- Each lesson has 3 age related craft activities.
- Everything you need is in the one book, so there is no need to buy children's activity books.
- Undated materials allow you to use the lessons to fit your situation without wasting materials.
- Once you have the entire syllabus, there is no need to repurchase.

Teacher's Challenge

Located throughout this book are cartoons highlighting some aspects of the Bible passages. Hidden in one or more of these cartoons is a bookworm (see box on right - not actual size).

If you consider yourself observant and want a challenge, count the number of times the bookworm appears in this edition. The correct answer is on the back page. Don't look until you are sure you have found them all!

Christmas Gifts

Week 1 NATIVITY PLAY

Week 2 GOD'S GIFT TO MARY *Luke 1:26-56*
To teach that Jesus was both man and God.

Week 3 GOD'S GIFT TO THE WORLD *Luke 2:1-20*
To teach that Jesus came to save us.

Week 4 GOD'S GIFT TO SIMEON *Luke 2:21-40*
To teach that Jesus is the promised Messiah.

Week 5 THE WISE MEN'S GIFTS TO JESUS *Matthew 2:1-12*
To teach that Jesus is to be worshipped.

Series Aims

1. To understand the stories in their context.

2. To understand that God loves us so much that he gave us Jesus to be our Saviour.

The Christmas story is a familiar one, but many of the younger children will not remember the details and some of the older ones will have picked up a mixture of fact and fantasy. So it is important to study the passage carefully and present the children with the facts and not a romanticised version.

The first week is a Nativity play, which can be used in a different slot or omitted if wished.

The second lesson deals with the angel coming to Mary to tell her she will have a baby. We need to convey the wonder and excitement she must have felt and to point out to the children that Jesus was both man and God and would be king of the Jews for ever.

In the third lesson we hear about the birth of Jesus and the angels giving the shepherds the good news of the birth of their Saviour.

The fourth lesson deals with Jesus being presented at the Temple in accordance with the Law, and Simeon's recognition of this baby as being the promised Messiah - not only for the Jews but also for the Gentiles (Luke 2:30-32).

The series ends with the story of the wise men coming to worship Jesus. So, even as a baby, we see Jesus worshipped by Jew and Gentile.

At Christmas all the children get excited about the presents they will receive. Try and instil into them a similar excitement about the present God gives to us - Jesus - and our need to respond in thankfulness and worship.

Memory Work

3-5s God so loved the world that he gave his only Son.

John 3:16

5-9s God so loved the world that he gave his one and only Son, that whoever believes in him shall not perish but have eternal life.

John 3:16

Some children are getting ready for Christmas and discussing what they like best about it. As they talk about God's present to us the Christmas story is acted out in front of them. The children acting the Christmas story mime the actions while the other children are telling the story.

Cast

2-5 children (number optional)
Angel Gabriel
Mary
Joseph
Innkeeper

Shepherds + toy sheep
Angels
3 Wise Men + pages (pages optional)
Herod
Extra innkeepers (optional)

Stage Set

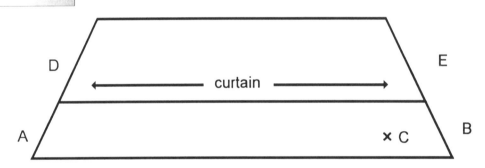

A star is required hanging above centre stage.

Play

[2-5 children enter at B and move to C where a Christmas tree is waiting to be decorated. They start to decorate the tree and wrap presents.]

Child 1 I love Christmas.

All So do I!

Child 2 What do you like best about Christmas?

Child 3 I like the Christmas tree with its tinsel and fairy lights.

Child 4 I like waking up on Christmas morning and finding a bulging stocking at the end of my bed.

Child 5 I like hanging up Christmas cards and opening the doors on my advent calendar.

Child 1 I like getting presents.

Child 2 Why do we give presents at Christmas?

Child 4 We give presents in memory of God's present to us.

Child 2 What was God's present to us?

Child 4 God became a man and was born as a baby at Bethlehem.

Child 2   How could God become a man?

Child 4   Well, it happened like this.   There was a young woman who lived in a town called Nazareth.   Her name was Mary and she was engaged to be married to a man called Joseph.

[*While child 4 is speaking Mary enters at B and moves to centre stage in front of the curtain.   Mary is dusting.*]

Child 4   One day an angel visited Mary in her home.

[*Angel Gabriel enters from the middle of the closed curtain.*]

Child 4   Mary was very frightened, but the angel said, 'Don't be afraid, Mary.   You have found great favour with God.   You are going to have a baby, a son, and you are to call him Jesus.'   Mary said, 'How can this happen to me?   I am not married.'   But the angel said, 'God's Holy Spirit will come upon you and God's power will rest on you.   For this reason your son will be called the son of God.'   Mary said, 'I am the Lord's servant.   May it happen to me as you have said.'

Song 1   **The Angel Gabriel from heaven came.**

[*Angel Gabriel exits through the middle of the curtain and Mary exits at B.*]

Child 2   If Mary lived in Nazareth, how did the baby come to be born in Bethlehem?

Child 5   The Roman Emperor of the time decided that he wanted to count all the people in his empire.   Everyone had to go to his family's home town.   Joseph was a descendent of King David so he had to go to Bethlehem.   He took Mary with him.   It was a long journey for someone expecting a baby.

[*Mary and Joseph enter at B and walk slowly across the stage, stopping at the far side.*]

Child 4   I expect she rode on a donkey.

Song 2   **Little Donkey.**

[*Place an Inn sign at the join of the curtain.*]

Child 2   Why was Jesus born in a stable and not in a house or hospital?

Child 5   When they got to Bethlehem it was packed full of people who had also come to be counted.   Joseph tried to find a place for them to stay, but all the inns he tried were full.

[*While child 5 is talking Joseph and Mary move around the stage "knocking" on doors.   Each time a man appears and shakes his head.   Eventually they knock at the door with the Inn sign.*]

Child 5   At last one innkeeper suggested that they might like to stay in his stable.   It was better than nothing.

[*The curtains open to reveal the stable scene with a manger in the middle.   Mary and Joseph follow the Innkeeper into the stable.   Innkeeper exits at E.*]

Child 5   While Mary and Joseph were staying there the time came for the baby to be born.   Mary gave birth to a son.   She wrapped him in strips of cloth and put him in the manger, where the animal food was usually put, because they didn't have a cot for him to sleep in.

[*Mary rearranges the baby in the manger so that it is more visible.*]

Child 2   That was a very strange place for such an important baby to be born.

Song 3   **The Calypso Carol.**

[Curtains close.]

Child 2   If the baby was born in a stable how did anybody get to know about it?

Child 3   There were some shepherds out in the fields looking after their sheep during the night.

[Shepherds enter from B and sit down centre stage.]

Child 3   Suddenly, an angel appeared to them and filled the night sky with God's glory.

[Angel Gabriel enters from A.]

Child 3   The shepherds were terrified but the angel said to them, 'Don't be afraid. I bring great and joyful news to you and all men everywhere. Today, in Bethlehem, your Saviour has been born. He is the Messiah. You will find him wrapped in strips of cloth and lying in a manger.'

[Angels enter from A.]

Child 3   Suddenly a great army of angels appeared, praising God saying, 'Glory to God in the highest and peace on earth to those with whom he is pleased.'

[Angels exit at A and move to back of stable scene behind Mary and Joseph.]

Child 3   The shepherds quickly decided to go to Bethlehem and see for themselves this great event.

[Shepherds get up and exit at A.]

Song 4   **How far is it to Bethlehem.**

[Curtains open to reveal stable scene.]

Child 3   The shepherds found Mary and Joseph and the baby Jesus just as the angel had told them.

[Shepherds enter at A and move to kneel in front of the manger.]

Child 3   They told Mary and Joseph what the angel had said and how they found the child. Mary and Joseph were amazed by what the shepherds said. The shepherds went back to the field, singing praises to God. It was just as the angel had told them.

[Shepherds exit at A. Curtains close.]

Child 2   Isn't there something about a star in the story, and some very strange presents the baby was given?

Child 1   Yes, there is. That's the bit of the story about the wise men who liked to study the night sky. One night they noticed a new star in the sky. They knew that this must mean that a new king had been born. They travelled to Jerusalem to the king's palace since they thought that would be the place to find him.

[While child 1 is talking the Wise Men and pages enter at B and Herod enters at A. The Wise Men and pages move towards Herod.]

Song 5   **Follow the Star verses 1 and 2.**

Child 1   King Herod was very worried when he heard the Wise Men's story. He thought this new king might take over his power and his palace. He did not know that Jesus' kingdom was in heaven, not on earth. Herod's experts in prophecy knew that the

Messiah would be born in Bethlehem so they told the Wise Men to try there. Herod asked them to let him know where to find the baby so he could go and worship him too - but he really wanted to kill Jesus so that he was not in any danger of losing his throne.

[Wise Men and pages exit at B and Herod exits at A.]

Song 5 **Follow the Star verse 3.**

[Curtains open during this verse to reveal the stable scene.]

Child 1 The Wise Men followed the star until it stopped over the place where Jesus was.

[Wise Men and pages enter at B and move to kneel in front of the manger.]

Child 1 They were delighted to find the baby Jesus with his mother Mary and they knelt down to worship him. Then they gave him 3 presents - gold because he was a king, frankincense because he was a priest, and myrrh because his death was going to be very important.

[Rest of cast enter quietly and position themselves around the baby.]

Child 2 Did the Wise Men tell King Herod where they found the baby?

Child 1 No. God warned them in a dream not to travel home that way.

Child 2 Did Herod try to kill baby Jesus?

Child 1 Yes, he did. But an angel warned Joseph in a dream to take his family to Egypt. The angels were still looking after him.

Child 2 But why did the angels rejoice when Jesus came if they knew that he would die? They weren't able to save him from **that** death.

Child 4 They rejoiced because Jesus was going to rescue men from the punishment for their sins. That's why the angels called him a saviour.

Child 2 Wow. God really has given us an amazing present in sending Jesus to be our saviour. What can we give to God this Christmas? What present could possibly be big enough?

Child 4 The Bible says we should give ourselves to him, to serve and obey him.

Child 5 To be part of his family.

Child 3 Then we can rejoice with the angels and join in the celebration.

Song 6 **Heaven invites you to a Party.**

[Curtains close.]

Carols

The Angel Gabriel from Heaven came
(Baptist Praise & Worship 177)
Little Donkey (Church Family Worship 644)
The Calypso Carol (Junior Praise 214)
How far is it to Bethlehem? (Carols for Choirs 2 p.66)
Follow the Star (Chappell of Bond St,
50 New Bond St, London W1Y 9HA)
Heaven invites you to a party (Makeway Music,
PO Box 263, Croydon, Surrey CR9 5AP)

Props

Christmas tree and decorations
Presents and wrapping paper
Duster for Mary
Inn sign
Baby wrapped in a shawl in box of straw
Wise men's gifts
Star

Preparation:
Read Luke 1:26-56, using the Bible study notes to help you.

Lesson aim:
To teach that Jesus was both man and God.

The gospels supply only limited details about the birth and early life of Jesus and the family of Mary and Joseph. This helps to prevent human interest from overshadowing the central aim of the gospels, which was not to write a biography, but to tell the history of the long-promised establishment of the Kingdom of God on earth.

1:26 The sixth month refers to Elizabeth's pregnancy.
Angel Gabriel is one of the two angels in the Bible who are named. He was also sent to Daniel to announce the Christ who was to come (Daniel 8:16; 9:21).

1:27 'Pledged' - this was as binding as marriage and could only be broken by divorce. It was in no way like our engagement. Bear in mind also that the concept of virgin birth is unique to Christianity. It has no parallel in other world religions and could never have been invented by contemporary Judaism, as it ran directly counter to all its preconceptions.

1:28 Mary is troubled not so much by seeing the angel but by what he has said, that she has been graciously chosen by God. Her reaction seems to indicate her unselfconscious humility and the deeply spiritual receptiveness of her heart. The announcement to Mary is contrasted with the announcement to Zechariah in that it was not in the solemn grandeur of the Temple that Gabriel now appeared, but in the privacy of a humble home at Nazareth.

1:32-35 Jesus is both Son of God (Son of the Most High) and son of man (of the line of David). He is conceived by the power of God yet born a child. Holy here means divine rather than morally pure.

1:34 Zechariah was disbelieving whereas Mary was puzzled. She understood that Gabriel meant without human intervention.

| 1:38 | Mary says she is God's servant (Greek = slave girl) and shows her complete obedience. This should not be underestimated. She would certainly carry a social stigma and suffer rejection by family and society, but she accepts God's will and is prepared to trust him. |

| 1:39 | The angel seems to have directed Mary to Elizabeth so that Mary could share her joy, both natural and supernatural. There must have been tremendous relief in being able to open her heart to another woman, in all things like-minded, when such openness was not yet possible within her immediate family. |

| 1:43-45 | 'My Lord ' shows that Elizabeth recognises Mary's child to be the Messiah. This is a personal understanding. John, her child, has to find out for himself and it is not until Jesus' baptism that he recognises Jesus as Messiah. |

| 1:46-48 | Mary's song is phrased largely in OT language. There are resemblances to Hannah's song (1 Samuel 2:1-10), but without the bitterness. There is also here a greater concentration on God's mercy. Mary knows she is a sinner and needs a Saviour. |

| 1:49 | Mary turns from thankfulness to think about God himself. She refers to three aspects of God's character: his power, his holiness and his mercy. |

Additional notes

Teaching this story to children today is made more difficult by their perception of the miraculous and what it means. Their daily diet from comics and the TV screen is fantasy and the supernormal. We need to ensure that they understand that the Bible story is fact not fiction. The familiarity of the story can also lessen its impact on us as teachers. The reality of the holy Son of God coming into our sinful world, 'taking the form of a servant, being born in the likeness of men' (Philippians 2:7), is staggering. It is the pivotal event in world history. It is not surprising, therefore, that Mary was overwhelmed when she realised she was to play a crucial role in this story.

Virgin birth. We should be sensitive to the levels of understanding of the children we are teaching. Emphasis should be on the fact of life rather than the facts of life!!

Lesson Plan

As this is the first proper lesson of the series, (the Nativity play may or may not have been performed),

you need to start with an introduction. The next 4 lessons are about different gifts, so you could start by asking the children if they like presents. What do they like about presents? When do they get them? When and why do they give them? In today's true story from the Bible we will learn about a very special present. Ask the children to listen very carefully to discover who gave the present, what the present was and who received it. Go over those questions at the end of the story and then teach the memory verse. Next week we will find out about someone else who received a present.

Visual aids

Make a frieze using flat figures or 3D figures. (For 3D figures see page 13.) Figures required - Mary, angel, Elizabeth.

Suggested layout for background:

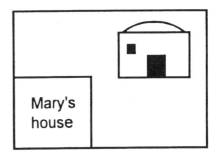

Start with Mary inside her house visited by the angel.

Then put Elizabeth in front of her house and move Mary to stand in front of Elizabeth's house.
For figures that need to move use bluetak to stick them onto the background.
Label the background with the class name at the top so that it is available for the next lesson.

Activities / 3 - 5s

The children will make an angel. Follow the instructions on page 14.

Activities / 5 - 7s

The children will make an angel. Follow the instructions on page 15.

The children will make small gift boxes from old Christmas/greetings cards. This is a traditional origami design. Read the instructions carefully and make one prior to the lesson to show the children. Remember, when doing a paper folding activity make sure every child has completed the first fold **before** you demonstrate the next one. Do steps 1 - 4 for both box top and box bottom for each child prior to the lesson.

Requirements

1 greetings card per child, pencil, ruler, scissors, glue stick.

The card must be a minimum of 11 cm across when folded. The larger the card, the easier it is to make the box.

The card front is the picture half.

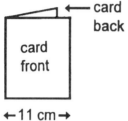

Instructions

1. Cut the card in half along the fold line.

2. Measure the card across and write the measurement on the card back.

3. Using that measurement, cut off the excess to make a square with the part of the picture you want visible on the box top in the centre.

4. On the back of the card front use a ruler to draw in diagonal lines.

5. In turn, fold in all 4 corners as follows:
   Fold corner into centre then fold c-d to e-f.

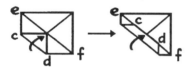

   Open out the card and repeat with the other 3 corners. Finish by opening out the card.

6. The card should now look like this (dotted lines indicate fold lines).

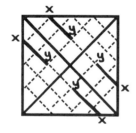

7. Cut along solid lines x-y.

8. Fold corner into centre. Fold again at f-g to make the side of the box. Fold in f-h and g-i to make ends. Do the same with point d.

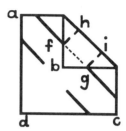

9. Fold point c over the end of the box with the point ending at the centre of the base. This secures the end flaps. Do the same with point a. A dab of glue may be required to hold the points down. The top of the box is now completed.

10. The bottom of the box is made in exactly the same

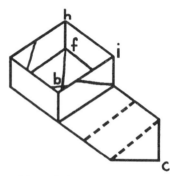

    way, but the sides of the square must measure 1 cm less than the square used for the box top (i.e. for a box with the top measuring 11 cm square before folding, the bottom before folding should be 10 cm square).

11. Write out the memory verse for each child on a piece of paper. This can be folded and placed in the completed box.

12. If the box is to be used for a decoration, make a hanging loop from gold string or thin ribbon and sellotape it to the top of the box.

Angel

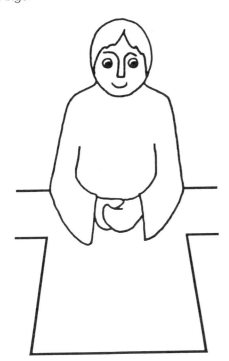

Mary and Elizabeth - give Elizabeth grey hair to show she is old.

line for figure with head-dress

Instructions

1. Fold sheet of A4 paper or card in half.

2. Draw 1 side of figure (as template).

3. Cut round drawn figure, including tab.

4. Open out and draw in detail of face, arms, etc.

5. Colour with bright pens.

6. Fold tabs and secure behind so that figure is 3D.

fold line

tab

fold line

fold line

Photocopy this page on card for each child. Prior to the lesson cut out the body, small wings and head. Fold the body into a cone and glue down the back.

Instructions

1. The children decorate the body with gold and silver stars, being careful not to cover the Bible verse around the bottom.
2. Bend the wings at the dotted lines, then cover with silver foil. Glue the wings to the back of the angel so that they face slightly backwards.
3. Colour the head then put the tab through the slot at the top of the body. Glue the bottom of the tab inside the body at the front.

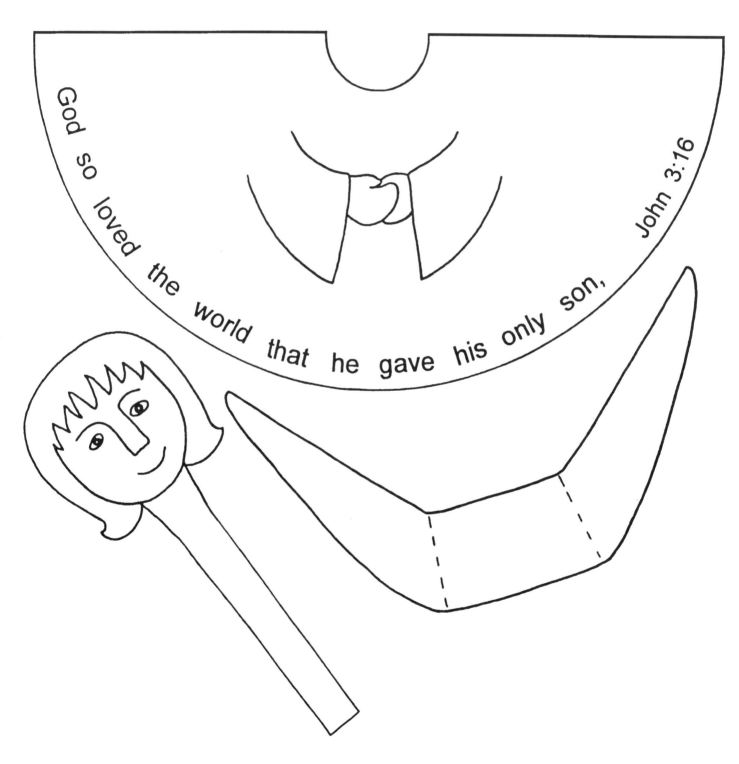

Each child requires pages 15 and 16 photocopied on card. Prior to the lesson cut out the body, arms, head and wings.

Instructions

1. Fold the body into a cone and glue down the back.
2. Glue the head tabs together and place over the top of the body, gluing in place.
3. Glue the arms to the back and sides of the body with the hands facing up.
4. Glue the wings to the back of the body.
5. Write the memory verse on a strip of paper, concertina fold and glue between the angel's hands. (The verse may need to be written out prior to the lesson.)
6. Decorate if time with gold and silver stars, pieces cut from doilies, etc.

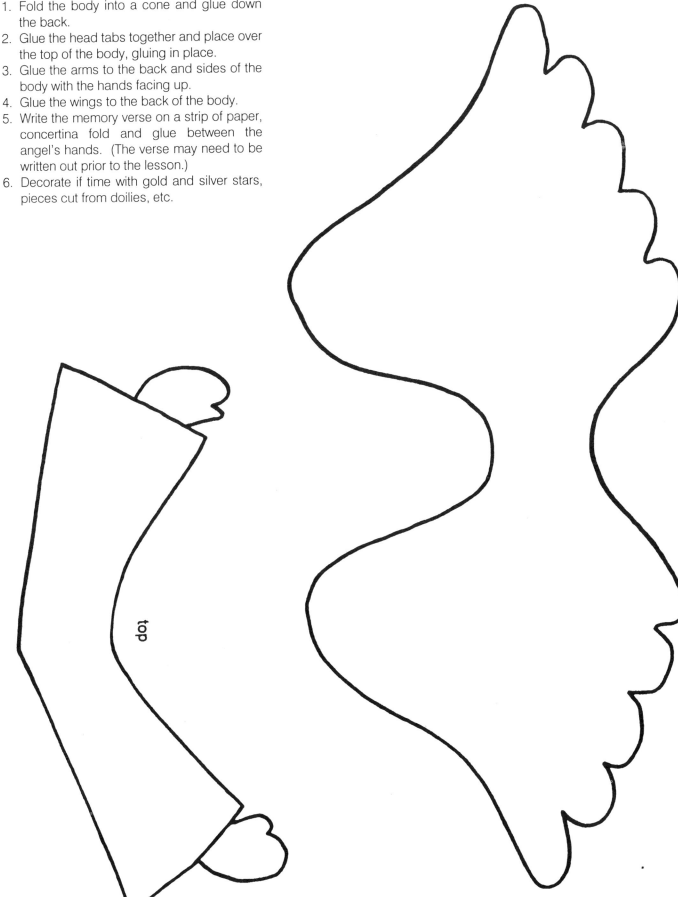

bottom

top

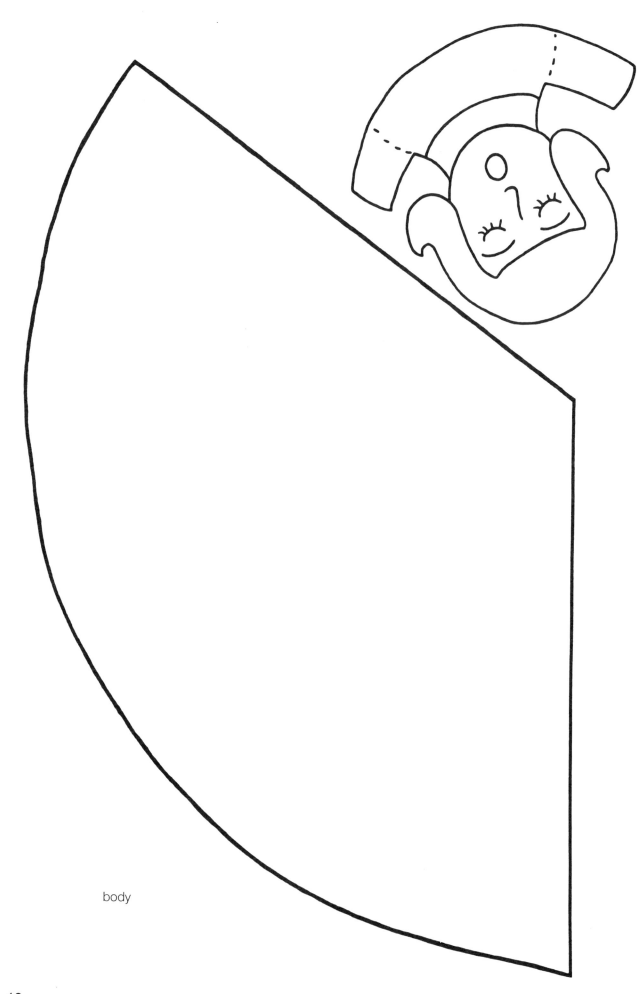

body

Preparation:

Read Luke 2:1-20, using the Bible study notes to help you.

Lesson aim:

To teach that Jesus came to save us.

2:1-3   The decree of a Roman Caesar was used by God to fulfil his purposes, revealed in the OT prophecies, that Jesus should be born in Bethlehem (Micah 5:2).

2:7   'Strips of cloth' - this was the normal way of wrapping a baby. The baby was placed diagonally on a square of cloth and 2 corners were turned over his body, one over his feet, and one under his head. The whole was then fastened by strips wound round the outside.

2:8   Shepherds were a rough group of men, often despised by more affluent people. They were not a group to whom it would be expected that God would reveal his son.

2:9   Cf. the Shekinah glory (Exodus 24:16, 1 Kings 8:10-11).

2:10   The good news was for all people, as promised years ago to Abraham (Genesis 12:2-3).

2:12   The shepherds were given explicit instructions as confirmation that this baby was the expected Saviour.

sort of people they would expect God to tell about the present. Stress that God loved the world, which includes the people they would consider outcasts, e.g. tramps, beggars. The gift of Jesus was for everyone, not just the 'nice' people. Finish by repeating the memory verse.

Visual aids

A wrapped present.

Build up a frieze using flat figures or 3D figures. (For 3D figures see pages 18 and 19, and the template on page 13.) You will need 2 backgrounds - 1 for the shepherds and sheep and 1 for the stable. The background for the shepherds consists of black sky with stars and green grass.

The stable scene needs a simple background (see diagram). Figures required are Joseph, Mary, baby in crib, angel, ox, donkey, sheep, shepherds. Use angel and Mary from last week.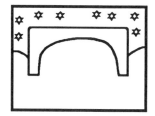

Move sheep and shepherds from the field background to the stable scene at the appropriate point in the story. Use bluetak to stick the figures to the background.

The Annunciation scene should still be set up for you to refer to. Put the class name above the stable background so that it will be kept for the next week.

Lesson Plan

Show the children a nicely wrapped present. Ask them who they give presents to. Recap on last week's story, going over who gave the present, what the present was and who received it. Revise the memory verse. In today's true story from the Bible we will hear about some other people who received presents. At the end of the story ask the children if the shepherds were the

Activities / 3 - 5s

The children will make a model of a baby in a crib. Each child requires page 20 photocopied on card plus half a sheet of A4 card to be a base. Follow the instructions on page 20.

Activities / 5 - 7s

The children will make a stable scene. Photocopy pages 21 and 22 on card for each child.

1. Colour and cut out the figures. Bend the tabs backwards.
2. Cut out the stands from page 22. Score and fold along dotted lines. Glue to the backs of the figures so that the figures stand up. The stands are labelled for each figure.
3. Arrange the figures on the base (remains of page 22) to make a nativity scene and glue in place. *"He gave his one and only Son,"* should be along the front of the scene.

Activities / 7 - 9s

The children will make a Christmas card. Each child requires page 23 photocopied on card and a bow made from ribbon or card.

1. Cut page 23 in half horizontally and fold the bottom half in half again to make the card.

2. Cut along the thick black line around three sides of the present and fold outwards along the dotted line.

3. Cut the remaining half of page 23 in half and glue the picture of the baby inside the front of the card so that the baby is visible through the 'opened' present.

4. Colour the card and write the memory verse inside.

5. Make a bow of ribbon or card and glue to the top of the present. When the bow is pulled the present will open.

6. For a card bow cut out the bow and strip from the remaining quarter of page 23. Wind the strip round the middle of the bow and glue.

Visual aids - 3D figures

See page 13 for the template for figures.

Mary

Shepherd
Draw one side of the figure (as template) plus shepherd's crook. Cut off the extra crook before drawing in the details of face, etc.

Joseph - as for the shepherd without a crook.

The manger can be flat, or folded like the figures with tabs from either end secured at the back.

Instructions

1. Fold a sheet of card 2" from the edge and cut out the heads of 1 ox, 1 donkey and as many sheep as required (see templates at the foot of this page).

2. Using the body templates cut out the required bodies.

3. The bodies are fixed flat to the background and the heads are glued to the front of the bodies with the heads facing forwards. The body can face in either direction.

4. For the donkey bend the ears forwards. For the ox bend the horns forwards.

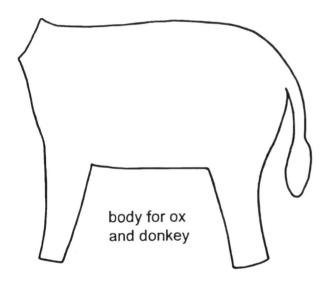

body for ox and donkey

body for sheep

fold line

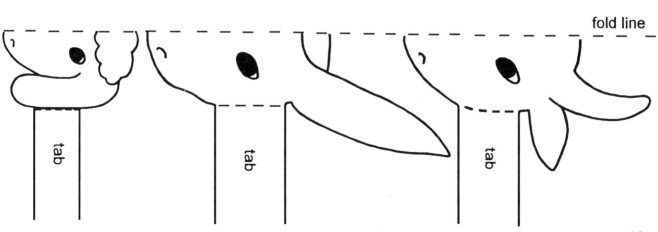

19

Prior to the lesson cut out a crib and a baby for each child. You will also need strips of material to wrap round the baby and to place inside the crib for bedding. Alternatively bedding could be made from straw or crumbled shredded wheat. Cut an A4 sheet of card in half to make 2 bases for the cribs. Write the memory verse along the front of each base.

1. Score and fold along dotted lines of the crib. Glue the larger tabs to the inside and the small tabs to the outside.

2. Colour the baby and wrap in strips of material.

3. Glue the crib to the base sheet and place bedding inside the crib. Put the baby on top of the bedding.

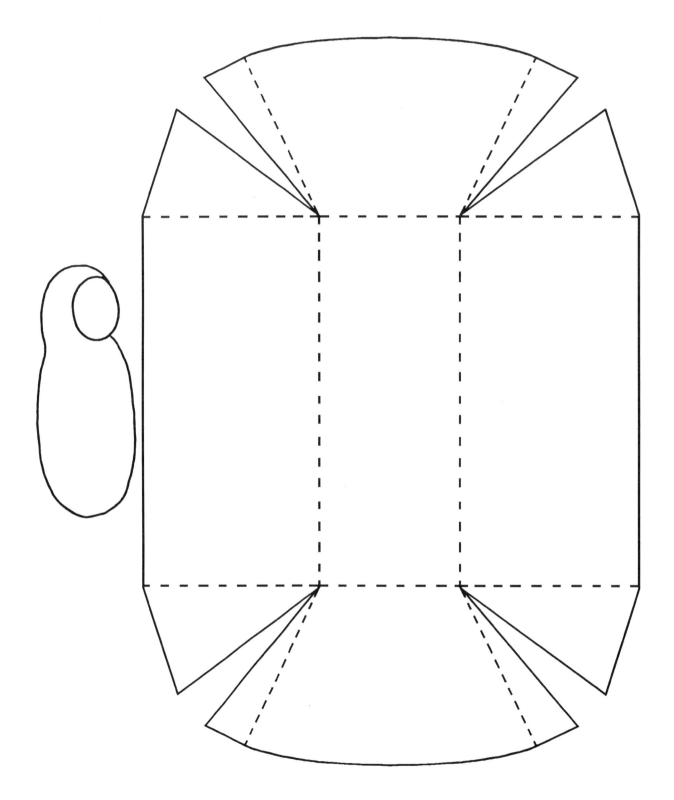

tab

tab

tab

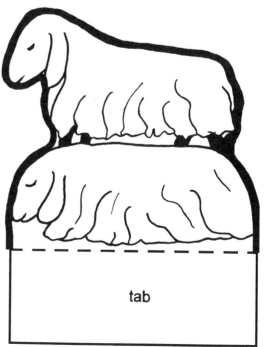

tab

God so loved the world that

he gave his one and only Son, that

perish but have eternal life. John 3:16

whoever believes in him shall not

Mary & Joseph		sheep
shepherds		manger

22

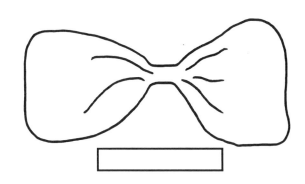

God's gift

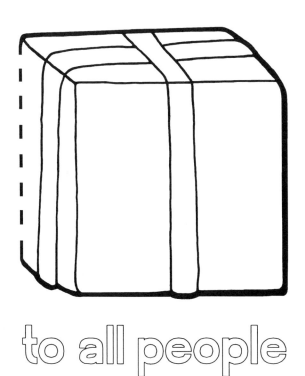

to all people

Preparation:
Read Luke 2:21-40, using the
Bible study notes to help you.

Lesson aim:
To teach that Jesus is the promised Messiah.

2:21   Jesus was circumcised on the 8th day, in accordance with the Law of Moses (Genesis 17:2, Leviticus 12:3). This was a sign that he was a member of God's covenant people and it placed him under the Law (Galatians 4:4).

2:22   Mary, according to the Law (Leviticus 12), was regarded as ceremonially unclean. For her purification she had to wait 40 days, then bring 2 purification sacrifices to the Temple - a lamb for a burnt offering and a pigeon for a sin offering. (Poor people were allowed to bring a second pigeon instead of the lamb - Leviticus 12:8.)

All first born sons belonged to God as a memorial of the Passover (Exodus 13:13-15, Numbers 18:15). Those born into the tribe of Levi were taken for service in the tabernacle (or temple). Those born into other tribes had to be redeemed (bought back) by their parents, who paid 5 shekels into the treasury.

Note on chronology
This story takes place after the birth of Jesus, but before the visit of the Wise Men. Mary and Joseph brought Jesus from Bethlehem to the Temple in Jerusalem, as was required by the Law of Moses. They then returned to Bethlehem, where they lived until the visit of the Wise Men and their subsequent flight to Egypt. This took place sometime between Jesus being 40 days old and 2 years.

Lesson Plan

This lesson will probably take place just before or just after Christmas. Start by talking about the presents they are hoping to receive / have received. Have they asked / did they ask for anything special? If so, what and will/did they receive it? Using the backgrounds and figures from the previous 2 weeks go over who received presents in those stories and what the presents were. Revise the memory verse. In today's true story from the Bible we will learn about someone who asked for a special present. Listen carefully so that you can tell me the name of the person, what the present was and whether the person got the present.

At the end of the story go over the questions and the memory verse. Next week we will learn about some people who gave presents.

Visual aids

Continue with the frieze using either flat figures or 3D figures. (For 3D figures see page 25 and template on page 13.) Figure of Joseph should be already in place on the previous weeks' backgrounds. Other figures required are Mary and baby, Simeon, Anna.

You will need 3 backgrounds - the annunciation and stable scenes should already be done. Refer to the annunciation and stable backgrounds as a lead in to to-day's lesson.

Background for Simeon and Anna - a plain sheet of paper with pillars drawn in to represent the temple courtyard. Label with the class name for use next lesson.

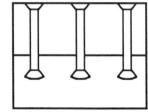

Simeon - as for the shepherd without the crook (see page 18 and template on page 13). Give him grey hair to show his age.

Mary with baby

Anna - as for Mary without the baby. Give her grey hair to show her age.

Activities / 3 - 5s

Photocopy page 26 and the baby on a strip from this page for each child. Prior to the lesson cut out the baby on the strip and cut along the thick black lines on Mary and Simeon. Thread the strip through the slits so that the baby moves from Mary to Simeon and back again. The children colour the picture.

Activities / 5 - 7s

Photocopy pages 27 and 28 back to back for each child. Fold in half to make a booklet. The children colour the booklet. Use it to revise the story.

Activities / 7 - 9s

The children will make a table decoration to remind them that Jesus came as the light of the world.

Requirements for each child

- 1 candle
- 1 yoghurt pot or disposable cup
- 1 piece of oasis to fit inside the container
- 1 strip of Christmas wrapping paper 5 cm wide and long enough to wrap round the outside of the container.
- sprigs of greenery, material or paper flowers, baubles, etc. for decoration. If you have no greenery holly leaves can be cut from green paper and attached to a tooth pick or pipe cleaner.
- the verse strip photocopied from the bottom of this page.

Instructions

1. Cut the top off the container to leave a base approximately 3.5 - 4 cm high.
2. Glue the strip of wrapping paper around the outside of the container, folding the excess in at the top.
3. Cut off the verse strip from the photocopied sheet and glue it around the outside of the container.
4. Place the piece of oasis inside the container and stick the candle in the middle.
5. Decorate by sticking bits of greenery, etc. into the oasis.

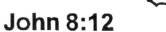

Jesus is the light of the world. John 8:12

Jesus, the promised Saviour

God so loved the world that he gave his only Son

John 3:16

God's gift to the world

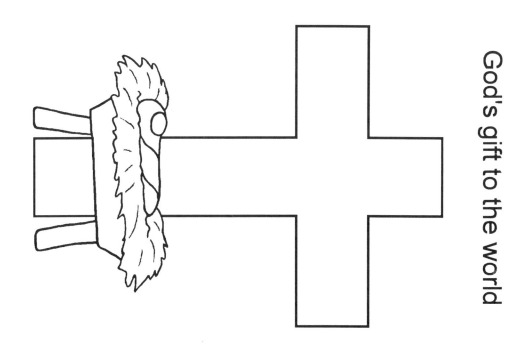

God so loved the world that he gave his one and only Son, that whoever believes in him shall not perish but have eternal life.
John 3:16

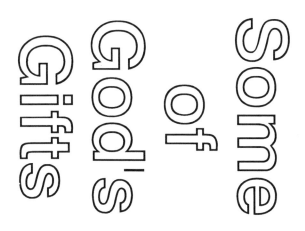

Some of God's Gifts

27

God's gift to Anna

God's gift to Simeon

Anna saw Jesus and gave thanks to God.

God promised Simeon that, before he died, he would see the Saviour of the world.

Preparation:
Read Matthew 2:1-12, using the Bible study notes to help you.

Lesson aim:
To teach that Jesus is to be worshipped.

Lesson Plan

In this story we see the Gentiles coming to worship Jesus (Isaiah 49:6, Luke 2:32)

2:1   Herod the Great (40-4 BC) was a puppet king under the Romans. Wise men (Magi) were astrologers and probably came from Persia or regions round about.
Jerusalem, the capital city, was the obvious place to go for information.

2:2   It was believed that a new star signified the birth of a great man.

2:3   Herod was known as a cruel man. If he was upset it was no wonder that the rest of Jerusalem was also upset!

2:4   Herod's question demonstrated that he had no doubt that it was to the Messiah the Wise Men were referring.

2:5-6   Cf. Micah 5:2.

2:7-8   Herod was already plotting how to get rid of the Messiah.

2:10   Cf. Numbers 24:17. The Jews interpreted this verse as a reference to the Messiah.

2:11   'House' - this episode took place some time between Jesus being 40 days old (Luke 2:22-24) and 2 years (Matthew 2:16), and common sense tell us that the family would not still be living in the stable.
The 3 gifts are the reason why the Wise Men are portrayed as 3 in number, although there is no definite evidence for this.
Psalm 72:10, Isaiah 49:7 - these verses explain why the Magi came to be thought of as kings.
The gifts - these were given as a mark of homage to a king. Gold signified kingship, frankincense divinity, and myrrh for a man who would die (myrrh was used in the embalming of bodies).

This is the last lesson in the series. Start the lesson by talking about the sort of presents we give. You need pictures of a man, a woman, a child and a baby. Point to the pictures one by one, asking the children what they would give to each person and why. Point out that people give presents that are suitable for the recipient. In today's story we will find out about the presents given to Jesus. Ask the children to listen carefully so that they can tell you what presents were given and why. Use the backgrounds and figures from previous weeks to revise the Christmas story to date.

At the end of the story find out what the children have learnt about the presents and the reason for giving them. Then pick out those same details from the preceding weeks. End with God's gift to the world, including us, and why that was appropriate - God's love for man, man's need of salvation and his inability to save himself. Revise the memory verse. Point out that Jesus was worshipped by both the shepherds (Jews) and the wise men (Gentiles). Ask what our response should be to God's gift and what we can give to Jesus.

Visual aids

Pictures of a man, woman, child and baby.

Continue with the frieze using either flat or 3D figures. (For 3D figures see pages 30 and 31 and the template from page 13.) You will need 2 backgrounds - 1 for the Wise Men following the star and the stable scene for your class from week 3. There should also be a background for the annunciation (week 2) and 1 for Simeon and Anna (week 4). Figures of Mary with the baby and Joseph should be available from last week. New figures required - 3 Wise Men, camels, star, Herod.

For the Wise Men's background you need a town scene to the left to represent Jerusalem. The Wise Men can travel to Jerusalem and meet Herod in front of it. Use to the stable scene for the home in Bethlehem, having removed the shepherds.

Wise men

Using the template on page 13 draw one side of the figure plus crown or turban. Follow the instructions with the template.

lesson cut out the box from page 32 and the lid from this page. Score and fold along the dotted lines. Use the box and lid shapes as templates to cut out pieces of wrapping paper for each child.

Activity time
1. Make up the box and lid by gluing the tabs to the outside of both.
2. Cover the box and lid with wrapping paper and glue in place.
3. Cut a piece of ribbon long enough to go round the box and glue to the bottom of the box. Place the memory verse written on paper in the box and put on the lid. Bring the ribbon over the lid and tie in a bow.

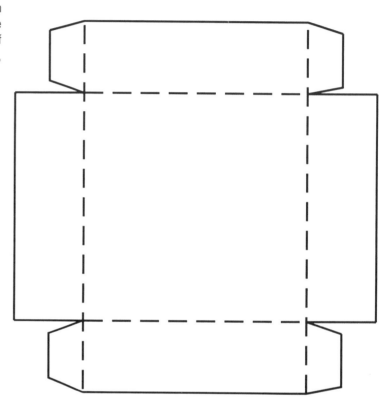

Activities / 5 - 7s

Photocopy pages 33 and 34 on card for each child. Follow the instructions on both pages.

Activities / 7 - 9s

Photocopy page 35 for each child on coloured card or paper, as dark as possible. Prior to the lesson cut out the hatched shapes using a craft knife. Each child also requires a sheet of greaseproof paper cut to A4 size. The greaseproof paper is glued to the back of the picture. From the right side of the picture colour the greaseproof paper appropriately, using felt tip pens. When the picture is held up to the light it will shine through the colours. The picture can be sellotaped to the bedroom window.

Activities / 3 - 5s

Photocopy page 32 and the box lid from this page on card for each child. You will also need Christmas wrapping paper, ribbon and a piece of paper with the memory verse written on it for each child. Prior to the

Fold a sheet of card 5.5 cm from the edge and cut out 3 heads using the template at the foot of this page. Cut out 3 bodies using the body template and make up as per the instructions for the animals on page 19.

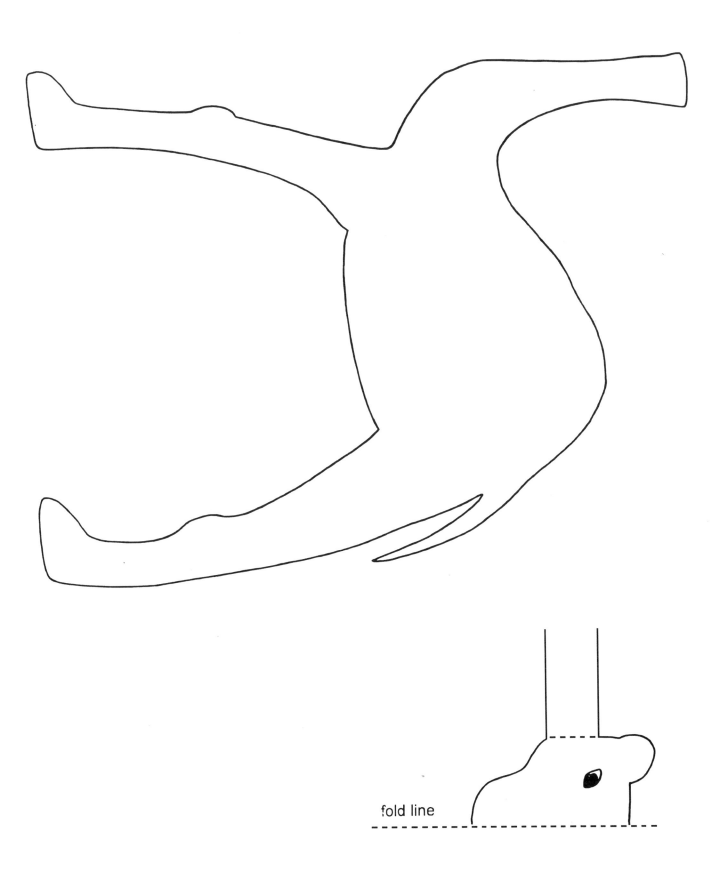

fold line

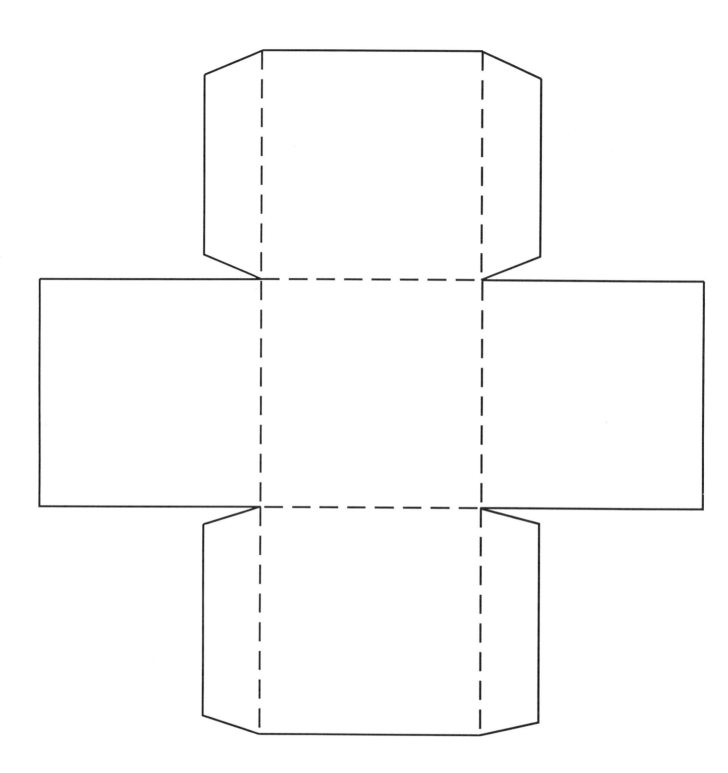

1. Fold this page in half along the dotted line and cut round the figure, including the tabs. This may need to be done before the lesson.

2. Open out the figure and colour.

3. Fold the tabs and glue together behind so that the figure will stand up.

4. Cut a slit up the middle at the bottom so that the wise man will sit on his camel.

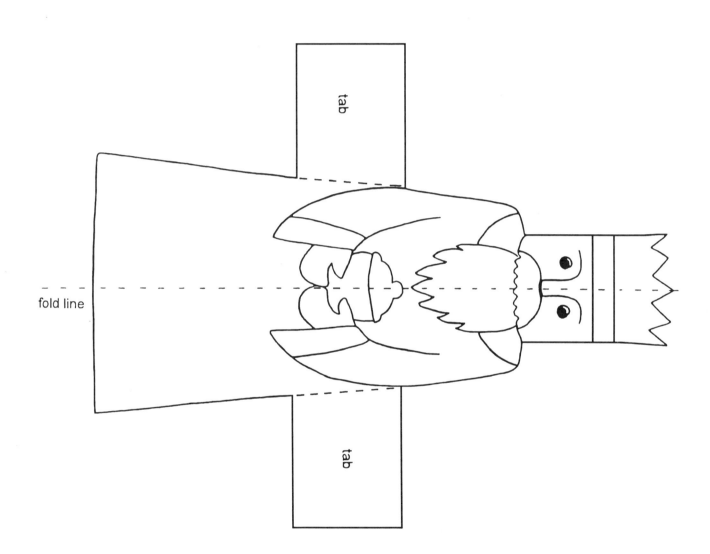

1. Fold the page in half along the dotted line.

2. Cut out the head, body and tail, being careful to cut through both layers of card and only along solid lines. This may need to be done before the lesson.

3. Glue the bottom end of the neck inside both ends of the front of the body.

4. Glue the ends of the tail marked X inside the rear ends of the body.

5. The camel should stand up.

Jesus' Authority

Week 6	AUTHORITY **OVER SIN**	*Mark 2:1-12*
	To teach that Jesus has power to forgive sins because he is God.	
Week 7	AUTHORITY **OVER DISEASE**	*Mark 3:1-6*
	To teach that Jesus has power over disease because he is God.	
Week 8	AUTHORITY **OVER NATURE**	*Mark 4:35-41*
	To teach that Jesus has power over nature because he is God.	
Week 9	AUTHORITY **OVER DEATH**	*Mark 5:21-43*
	To teach that Jesus has power over death because he is God.	
Week 10	AUTHORITY **OVER DEMONS**	*Luke 8:26-39*
	To teach that Jesus has power over demons because he is God.	
Week 11	AUTHORITY **TO FEED**	*Mark 6:30-44*
	To teach that Jesus has power to provide what is needful because he is God.	
Week 12	AUTHORITY **TO SAVE**	*Luke 19:1-10*
	To teach that Jesus has power to save men because he is God.	

Series Aims

1. To understand the stories in their context.

2. To learn that Jesus has authority and is to be obeyed.

During Jesus' life on earth devout Jews were looking for the Messiah - the one who would come from God to redeem his people and judge his enemies. This Messiah was to be a great King (Isaiah 9:6-7, Psalm 2), as well as a servant (Isaiah 42:1-4, Isaiah 53). At this time in history the Jews were a conquered nation, oppressed by the Romans. It was no wonder, then, that they looked for a kingly Messiah, who would drive out the Romans from their land.

At Christmas we saw the baby Jesus welcomed as the promised Messiah by Simeon (Luke 2:21-40) and worshipped by Gentile wise men (Matthew 2:1-12). In this series we will study 7 of the miracles Jesus performed which demonstrated his authority (or kingship).

The first lesson looks at the healing of the paralytic and Jesus' authority to forgive sin. In the second lesson Jesus heals the man with the withered hand and, by so doing, comes into conflict with the religious authorities. The third lesson deals with Jesus stilling the storm and the resultant response of his disciples, 'Who is this man? Even the wind and the waves obey him?'

The fourth and fifth lessons study Jesus' authority over death (the raising of Jairus' daughter) and demons (healing the demoniac), both of which point to his divinity. In the sixth lesson we see Jesus' great compassion for the hungry crowd and his ability to provide for their needs. The last lesson on the series looks at the conversion of Zaccheus and the resultant change in his behaviour.

By the end of this series the children should recognise that Jesus is truly God and, therefore, king of this world.

Memory Work

3-5s   Jesus Christ is Lord.

Philippians 2:11

5-9s   Jesus said, "I have been given all authority in heaven and on earth."

Matthew 28:18

Preparation:
Read Mark 2:1-12, using the Bible study notes to help you.

2:3   The man, being paralysed, was totally dependent on his friends to take him to Jesus.

2:4   The friends were not deterred by the difficulties and they were not prepared to wait until a more convenient moment. The houses had flat roofs. The roof would have been made by laying branches and other bits of vegetation over the beams and then packing a thick layer of earth tightly on top, which would then be rolled or plastered to help shed the rain. It would have been fairly easy to make a hole in it (and fairly easy to repair afterwards!).

Lesson aim:
To teach that Jesus has power to forgive sin, because he is God.

2:5   Jesus responds to the man's spiritual need before responding to his physical need. Which was the most important to Jesus and which to the man?

2:7   The teachers of the Law were correct - only God can forgive sin.

2:8-11   Jesus responds to their unspoken criticism by demonstrating his authority to forgive sin - he tells the man to get up and walk.

2:10   'Son of Man' is a title used in Daniel 7:13-14 to refer to the Messiah. Jesus used the title to refer to himself over 50 times.

Lesson Plan

This is the first lesson of a seven week series and it is important from the outset to ensure that the children understand what it means to have authority (the power/right to enforce obedience). You might like to start by playing *Simon Says*. When a child does the wrong movement they should miss at least one turn. Talk to the children about what happened when they disobeyed your instructions. Why were you able to make them miss a turn? Proceed by holding/pinning up pictures of people who have authority over them, e.g. parent, teacher, policeman, king or queen. Use the pictures to reinforce what it means to have authority. In today's true story from the Bible we will find out about someone who had power over something. Ask the children to listen carefully so that they can tell you who had the authority and over what.

At the end of the story go over the questions. Point out that the teachers of the law were right when they said only God can forgive sins. Ask the children how they know Jesus was able to forgive sins, (the man was able to get up and walk), and what this means about Jesus. Teach the memory verse.

Visual aids

Pictures of people who have authority over us, e.g. parent, teacher, policeman, king/queen.
Yoghurt pot people and a house made from a cardboard box are appreciated by the younger ones for the Bible story (see page 39).

Activities / 3 - 5s

Photocopy page 40 on card for each child. Prior to the lesson cut along the line to the right of the steps to remove the bed strip and paralysed man. Cut along the line between the man and the bed to leave a strip of card with a bed at one end. Cut out the man and attach him to the bed strip at the dots using a split pin paper fastener. Cut a slot along the thick black line to the left of the steps.
The children colour the picture and the man. Slot the bed strip through the slot to the left of the steps. Start with the bed strip at the top of the slot then lower it to the floor. The man can be swivelled to a standing position to show what happened when Jesus healed him.

Activities / 5 - 7s

Each child requires page 41 photocopied on card, a paper clip and approximately 20 cm fine string. Prior to the lesson cut out the shapes on page 41 and score and fold along the dotted lines. Cut along the solid black lines around the door and hole in the roof.

Activity time
1. Glue the house front to the house sides with the people inside.

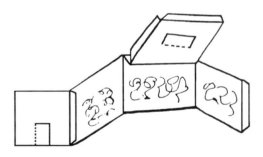

2. Fold the roof tabs up and glue the roof to the walls, leaving a parapet around the roof.
3. Draw on steps and a window. Open the door and roof flap.
4. Sellotape the paper clip to the back of the stretcher. Tie the string to each end of the paper clip to make a long loop.
5. Fold the friends with their legs behind them and glue them to the roof facing the open flap.

6. Lower the stretcher through the hole in the roof. Watch by peeping through the door.
It is helpful to make one before the lesson to show the children.

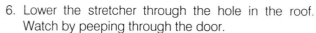

Activities / 7 - 9s

Over the seven lessons of this series the children will make a book about Jesus demonstrating his authority over various things. Each week the children need to understand what Jesus has power over, and what this means to them personally, e.g. the first lesson shows Jesus' power to forgive sin. A 7-9 year old should be able to understand that this means a) they can come into a relationship with God, and b) they can be free from guilt for sins that have been confessed.

Each child requires page 42 photocopied on card, a sheet of A4 card for the back cover, pages 43, 44, 45, 46 and 47 photocopied on paper and an A4 slide binder to hold the book together.

Prior to the lesson prepare page 46 as follows:
* Cut along the solid lines around the windows so that the children can fold them back along the dotted lines.
* Cut off the bottom strip from page 47.
* Glue page 47 behind page 46, lining up the tops of the pages, so that the pictures can be seen through the open windows.

Put the pages in the book in numeric order, omitting page 45.

1. Start the lesson by reminding them that Simeon recognised Jesus as the promised Messiah (week 4 - Luke 2:25-35)).
2. Use the word square on page 43 to help explain who the Messiah was and what he came to do. It is helpful to have a large version of the word square on a board so that this can be done as a joint activity. Only go on to the next word once all the children have marked off the first word in their books. This helps prevent the less able children falling behind.
3. Discuss what it means to have authority and how God's authority differs from human authority (God is all-knowing, all-powerful and does not make mistakes).
4. See if the children can think of ways Jesus demonstrated his authority whilst on earth.
5. Open window 1 on page 46. Ask the children to guess what story this refers to. If they do not know, progress to window 2, then window 3.
6. Following the story the children glue 'heals the paralysed man' in the rectangle at the top of page 46 and fill in the gaps in the sentence at the bottom.
7. Cut out the appropriate symbol from page 45 and glue it onto the map on page 44. Draw an arrow from the symbol to the place where the miracle occurred.
The activity books and map symbols stay at Sunday school until the end of the series.

House Take a large cardboard box and cut out a door and a window. Cut flaps in the top that can be pushed open to lower the paralysed man on his stretcher.

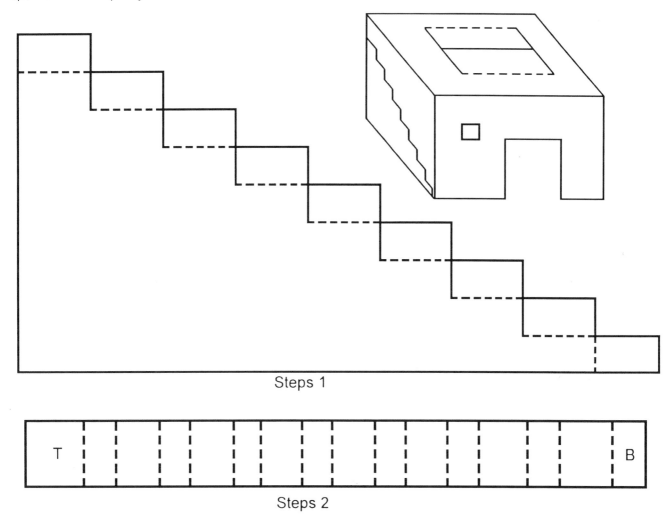

Steps 1

Steps 2

Stairs Take a piece of card the same size as the side of the house and draw in the steps, starting at the back and an inch below the top and ending at the bottom and an inch from the front. Then draw in a second zigzag line an inch above the first (see diagram). Cut out along the upper line, cutting down to the lower line along the solid lines as on the diagram. The dotted lines on the diagrams are fold lines. Cut out a strip of card one inch wide and concertina fold to fit the zigzag line of the steps. Attach the strip of card to the top of the folded over prongs of steps 1 with staples. Attach the finished steps to the side of the house using large split pin paper fasteners.

People You need yoghurt pots or plastic drinking cups, egg cartons, scraps of material, wool, rubber bands, cotton wool, sellotape, glue, pens. Cut the head from an egg carton and sellotape onto a yoghurt pot or plastic cup. Draw on a face. Dress with a piece of material secured round the middle with wool or a rubber band. Tuck the bottom edge of the material inside the bottom of the pot. Attach the head-dress in similar fashion to the robe. Glue on cotton wool as a beard if required.

Make a stretcher from the lid of a margarine tub.
Attach string to the 4 corners so that the paralysed man can be placed on the stretcher and lowered into the house through the roof flaps. Place a piece of material on the stretcher so that the man can roll it up and take it home.

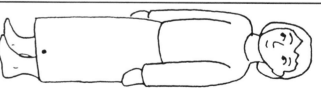

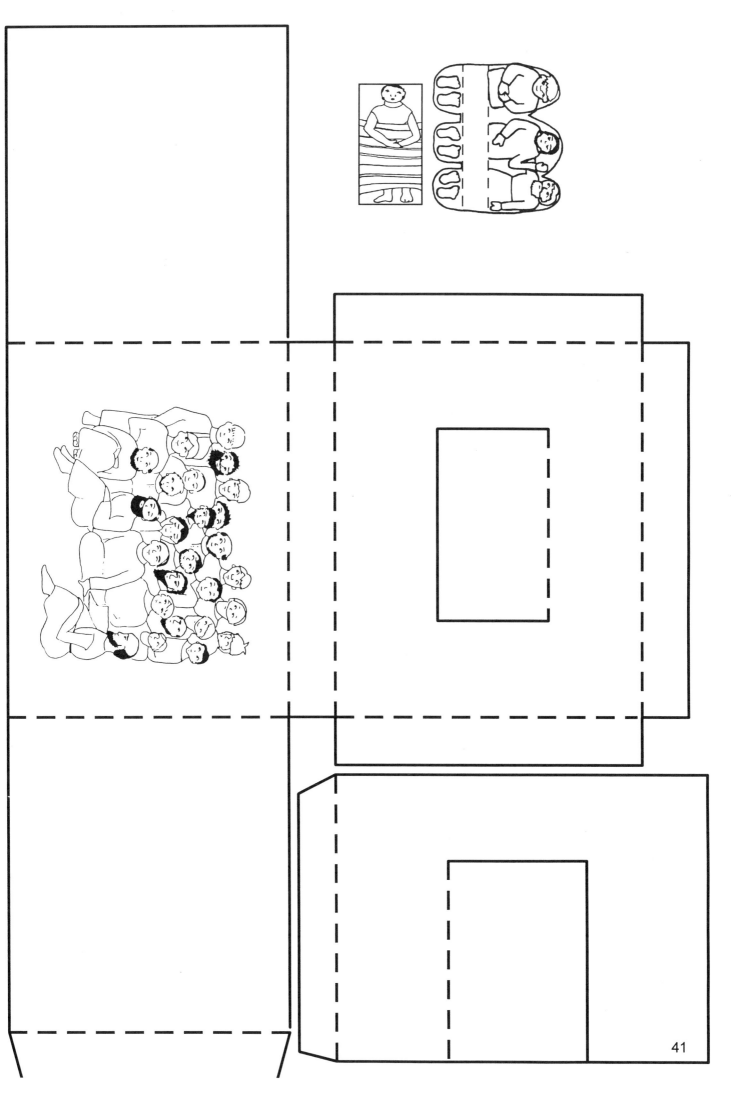

41

Jesus demonstrates his authority

W O R D S E A R C H

Can you find the following 10 words in the word square? The words read in a straight line forwards, downwards and diagonally. No letter is used more than once.

k	a	m	e	s	s	i	a	h	s
b	i	c	f	j	j	d	h	u	m
s	g	n	k	n	p	e	s	e	i
e	l	r	g	i	m	e	w	o	r
r	q	e	s	u	j	r	v	s	a
v	w	d	j	p	o	w	e	r	c
a	x	e	t	u	y	a	d	f	l
n	b	e	e	h	d	g	g	d	e
t	i	m	j	n	r	g	o	k	s
l	o	s	m	v	t	g	e	z	p

God

Jesus

Jews

judge

King

Messiah

miracles

power

redeem

servant

Once you have found all 10 words, use them to fill in the gaps in the sentences below.

During ....' life on earth, devout .... were looking for the .... - the one who would come from God to .... his people and .... his enemies. This Messiah was to be a great .... (Isaiah 9:6-7), as well as a .... (Isaiah 42:1-4). These seven .... that Jesus performed show that his .... is greater than any man's; his power is the power of ....

Palestine in the time of Jesus

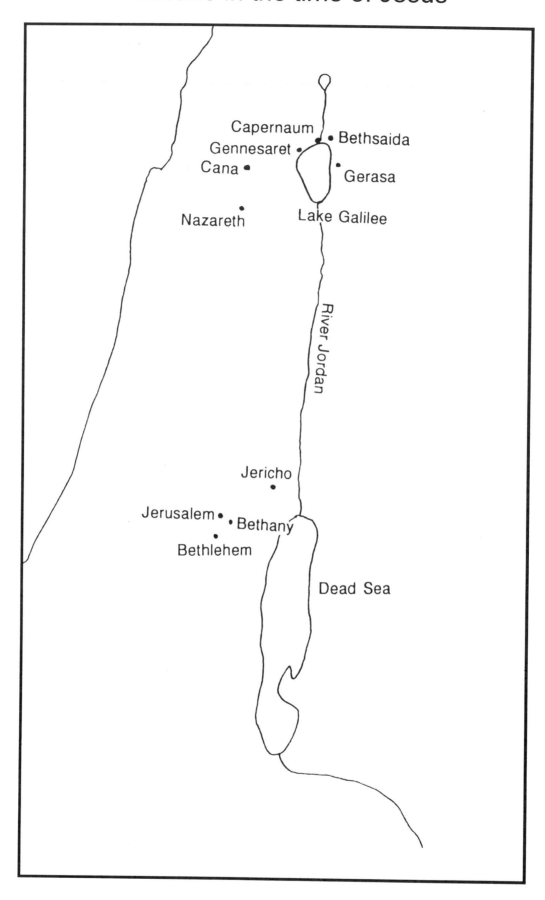

Symbols for use with the map

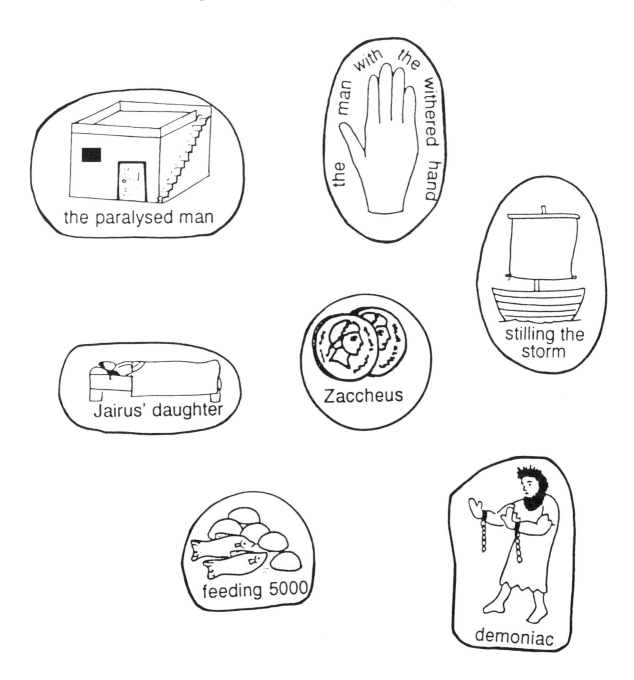

the paralysed man

the man with the withered hand

stilling the storm

Jairus' daughter

Zaccheus

feeding 5000

demoniac

Jesus

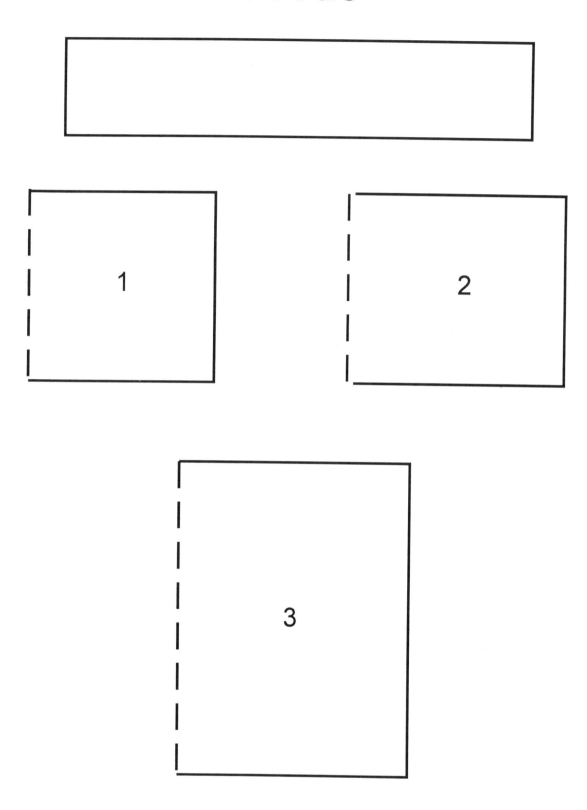

Jesus has power to   _ _ _ _ _ _ _ _ _ _ _ _ _ _ _ .

What does this mean to me?

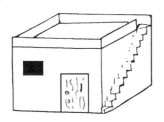

heals the paralysed man
Mark 2:1-12

Preparation:
Read Mark 3:1-6, using the
Bible study notes to help you.

Lesson aim:
To teach that Jesus has power over illness,
because he is God.

Lesson Plan

It is helpful to read Mark 2:23-28 as a prelude. Especially note Mark 2:27.

3:1   The man was in the synagogue on the Sabbath day - perhaps he thought religious people would be helpful? Luke 6:6 tells us that it was the right hand that was paralysed, the one that was most useful. Without full use of both hands he would have been unable to follow a trade, so may have been dependent on charity.

3:2   The verb used for 'watched him closely' indicates hostile observation.

3:3-4   Jesus gives the watchers a chance to observe the man's plight and respond with compassion. They were so keen on upholding the letter of the Law that they forgot the principle of love that runs through it; love of God for man and of man for God and his neighbour. For OT teaching on the Sabbath see Genesis 2:2-3, Exodus 20:8-11; 31:12-17, Leviticus 23:3, Deuteronomy 5:12-15, Nehemiah 13:16-22, Isaiah 58:13-14.
Do give careful thought to the subject of Sunday activities/work, especially those teaching the older groups.

3:5   Even though the man had not asked for healing, he had to respond to Jesus in order to get it. 'Became well' implies a change in appearance as well as in function.

3:6   The Herodians were the secular party and normally the Pharisees would have had nothing to do with them.

Remind the children of the meaning of authority (the power/right to enforce obedience). Go over last week's story, looking at what Jesus has authority over, how he demonstrated that and what it tells us about Jesus (he is God). Revise the memory verse. Ask the children if any of them have been ill. Did they go to the doctor? How were they made better? Did the cure happen immediately? For the younger children you might like to have a doll or teddy with a bad hand that needs to be bandaged. Ensure that the children realise that healing takes time and often requires medicines, etc. In today's true story from the Bible we will find out about someone Jesus made better. Ask the children to listen carefully so that they can tell you what was wrong with the man and how Jesus healed him (with a word).

After the story go over the questions. Point out that Jesus did what no doctor can do in restoring a wasted hand. You might want to point the older children back to creation and how God said the word and it happened. Stress the lesson aim.

Visual aids

Stand up figures, so that the sick man can come out from the crowd and stand before Jesus. Figures should be mounted on card with a tab at the feet that can be bent backwards. If necessary a piece of card can be attached at the back of the head and to the tabs, to give more rigidity.

Figures required are Jesus, a crowd of people, the man, a couple of Pharisees (optional). The man with the withered hand needs a movable arm (see activity for 3-5s).

Activities / 3 - 5s

Photocopy page 50 on card for each child. Prior to the lesson cut out the shapes and pierce the black dots with a compass point or thick needle.

The children colour the shapes. Make the withered arm by joining the pieces together with split pin paper fasteners as shown.

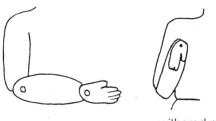

withered position

Finally glue the stand to the back of the figure so that he can stand up.

Activities / 5 - 7s

The children will make a booklet. Photocopy pages 51/52 and 53/54 back to back for each child. Fold the pages in half and staple at the fold, checking that the pages are in numeric order 1 - 8.

Go through the booklet as a class activity. The children draw a picture of the man in the square on the front cover and colour the booklet if time allows.

Activities / 7 - 9s

The children continue with the activity book. Photocopy page 55 on card and page 56 on paper for each child. Page 55 is used to make a decoder and page 56 is added to the back of the activity book. The page containing the map symbols should be with the activity book.

Following the story,
- cut out the appropriate symbol from page 45 and glue onto the map. Draw an arrow from the symbol to the place where the miracle occurred (in the region of Capernaum).
- make the decoder, following the instructions on page 55. Use it to decode the memory verse on page 56. Start learning the verse.
- answer the questions page 56, doing this as a class activity. Do give some thought to the answers **before** the lesson.

The activity books stay at Sunday school until the end of the series.

stand

Jesus heals a man with a withered hand

Mark 3:1-6

1

Jesus said

'I have been given all authority in heaven and on earth.'

Matthew 28:18

8

What would you miss most if you didn't have strong, healthy arms and hands?

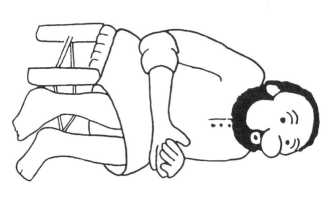

2

How could you use your hands to say thank-you to God for health and strength?

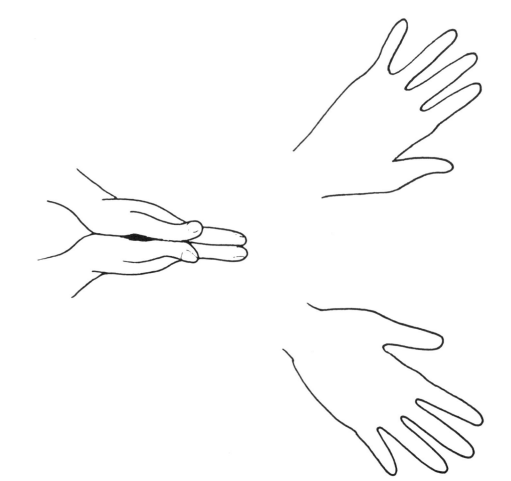

7

52

Would it be climbing trees and swinging?

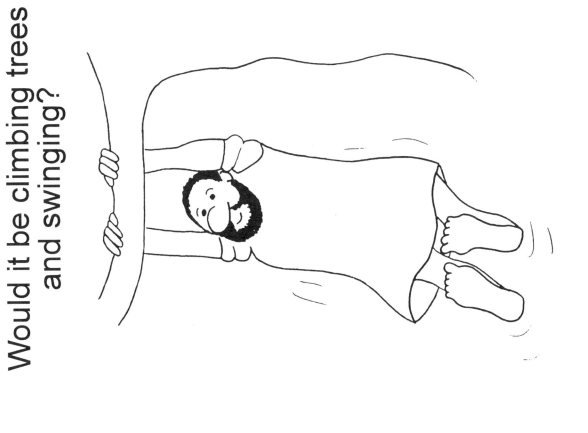

.... or something else?

3

What might the man do to say thank-you?

6

Write a list or draw pictures
to show what it would be.

Why do you think Jesus
healed the man's hand?

Secret Decoder

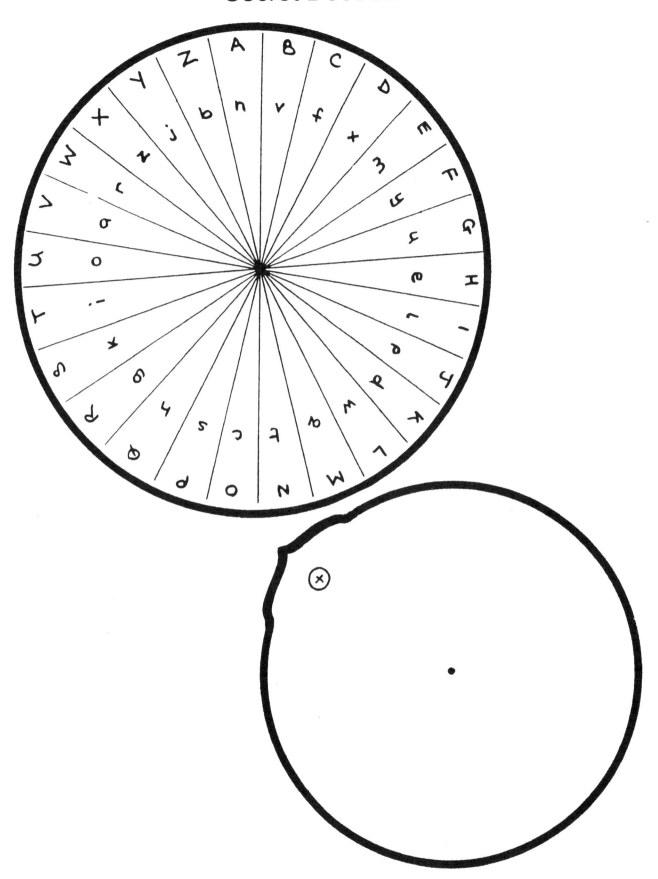

Cut out both discs. Punch a hole at X. Attach the small disc on top of the large disc using a split pin paper fastener through the centre. Make sure that the 2 discs rotate independently.

Jesus heals the man with a paralysed hand.
Mark 3:1-6

Jesus knew what was in men's hearts (Mark 2:8) because he is God. Make a secret decoder and use it to decode the memory verse. Turn the inner dial until the letter you want appears in the hole. Then the pointer will point to the decoded letter.

<pre>
_   _ _ _ _   _ _ _ _   _ _ _ _ _
l   e n a m   v m m t   u l a m t

_ _ _   _ _ _ _ _ _ _ _   _ _
n w w   n o i e c g l i j   l t

_ _ _ _ _ _   _ _ _   _ _   _ _ _ _ _
e m n a m t   n t x   c t   m n g i e
</pre>

Matthew 28:18

Jesus had power over _ _ _ _ _ _ _ .

Does this mean:

1. I need never be ill?

2. If I am ill, it is because I have done something wrong?

3. If I am ill I should ask God to make me better?

4. If I go to the doctor it means I don't have faith in God?

WEEK 8
Authority Over Nature

Preparation:
Read Mark 4:35-41, using the
Bible study notes to help you.

Lesson aim:
To teach that Jesus has power over nature,
because he is God.

Mark 4:1-2 sets the scene.

4:37   The hills around Lake Galilee act as a funnel
        for the winds, which arise suddenly and
        unpredictably, whipping up the water and
        causing great trouble for people in boats.

4:38   Jesus had been teaching all day and was
        tired (Mark 4:1-34).

4:39   Jesus gave the command himself, he did
        not ask God to do it, thus demonstrating his
        authority as Creator.
        When the wind stops, waves take a long
        time to calm down. In this case there was
        complete calm. It could not, therefore, have
        been a coincidence.

4:41   Note the disciples' response.

Lesson Plan

Start by reminding the children of the meaning of
authority (the power to enforce obedience). Go over
the previous 2 lessons, bringing out what Jesus has
authority over, how his authority was demonstrated and
what this teaches us about Jesus - he is God. Revise
the memory verse. Tell the story using the paper boat.
At the end of the lesson stress the lesson aim. Remind
the older children of how God created everything with a
word. In the light of who Jesus is, discuss with the
children what response is required from them.

Visual aids

Make a boat from brown paper (see page 59). It will
float in a bowl of water (better without the mast). The
bowl can be rocked to get the 'waves' going and the
children can blow to be the wind. You can
demonstrate to the children how long it takes for the
waves to stop once you stop causing them, and point
out the miracle that, **at Jesus' word**, they stopped
immediately.

Activities / 3 - 5s

Each child requires page 60 photocopied on card, a
piece of blue gummed paper approximately 6" square,
a piece of dark blue tissue paper 8-10" square, bluetak
and sellotape. Prior to the lesson cut out the boat and
verse strip from page 60.

Instructions

1. Scrunch up the tissue paper, lick the gummed paper and stick the tissue paper to the gummed side to form the rough sea. The blue side of the gummed paper is the calm sea.
2. Fold the boat along the dotted lines with the people visible on the outside (see diagram).
3. Glue the memory verse strip to one side of the boat.
4. Stick the bows and stern together with sellotape.
5. Use bluetak to stick the boat onto the rough or the calm sea.

Activities / 5 - 7s

Each child requires page 61 photocopied on paper, an A4 sheet of blue paper and a split pin paper fastener.

Instructions

1. Place the A4 sheet of blue paper on the table with the longer sides at the top and bottom. Draw steep waves along the bottom half of the page. Turn the page round and draw calm waves along the bottom half of the page (see diagram).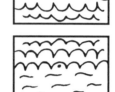
2. Cut out the boat from page 61, cutting along the thick black line.
3. Attach the boat to the middle of the sheet of blue paper using a split pin paper fastener through the black dot at the middle of the boat. The boat can be swivelled round to show it riding on a rough sea or a calm sea.
4. Cut off the verse strip from page 61 and glue it below the boat on the calm sea.
5. Colour the boat.

Activities / 7 - 9s

The children continue with the activity books. Photocopy pages 62, 63 and 64 for each child. Prior to the lesson cut along the solid lines around the windows on page 62 so that the children can fold them back along the dotted lines. Cut off the bottom strip from page 63 and glue page 63 behind page 62, lining them up from the top, so that the children can see the pictures through the opened windows. Add pages 62/63 and 64 to the back of the activity books. The page containing the map symbols should be with the activity books.

Lesson time

Before the lesson think about what sort of things make the children afraid, e.g. darkness, bullying, getting things wrong at school, dangerous situations, natural phenomena.

What should they do about these things? The disciples took their problem to Jesus and so should we. Also give some thought to the practical things which might help them.

You should also give some thought to 'Why does God allow earthquakes?' etc. in case this is raised by the children.

1. Ask the children to open the first window on page 62 and guess what the story is about. If they do not know progress to window 2, then to window 3.
2. Tell the story.
3. The children glue the story title (cut from the bottom of page 63) into the rectangle at the top of page 62 and fill in 'nature' in the blanks at the bottom of the page.
4. Review the memory verse.
5. Fill in page 64. This should be done as a class activity.
6. Cut out the appropriate symbol from page 45 and glue to the map. Draw an arrow from the symbol to where the miracle took place.
7. If time make the origami boat (see page 59) and write the memory verse on the sail. Make sure that everyone has completed the first fold before progressing to the next.

The activity books stay at Sunday school until the end of the series.

1. Crease a square of paper along the diagonals and unfold again.

2. Fold the four corners to the centre.

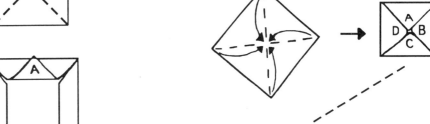

3. Fold points A and C backwards on top. Tuck points B and D underneath.

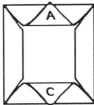

4. Turn the boat through 90° left, then fold sides X and Y under along dotted lines to centre,

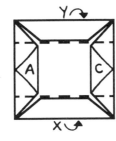 to look like this.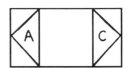

5. Turn model over.

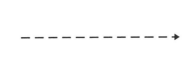

6. Fold the four corners inwards.

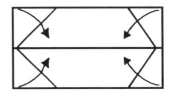

7. Fold points A, B, C and D to centre; the creases will come approximately along the dotted lines shown. Press Folds.

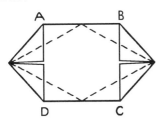

8. Fold X and Y to the centre. Crease firmly.

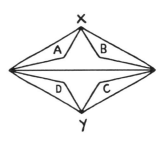

9. Placing fingers under the middle slit, gently lift and raise the sides, at the same time turning the model over.

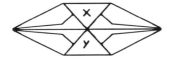

10. Press in with the thumbs and the fingers and pull up the sides, thus turning the model inside out.

11. Make a mast by rolling a narrow strip of paper spirally into a tube, gluing the end and trimming to a point. Cut to length required and fix to boat by slitting the base and splaying out, gluing the tabs formed.
    Curve a square of paper, to the right size, fold down edges and glue to mast for a sail.

    This boat will actually float!

Jesus Christ is Lord

Philippians 2:11

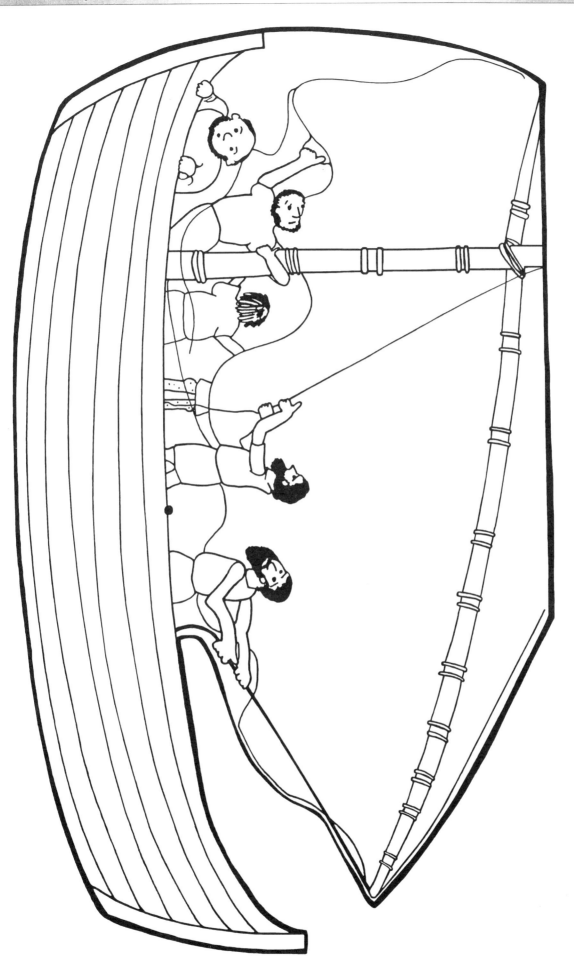

Jesus said, "I have been given all authority in heaven and on earth." Matthew 28:18

Jesus

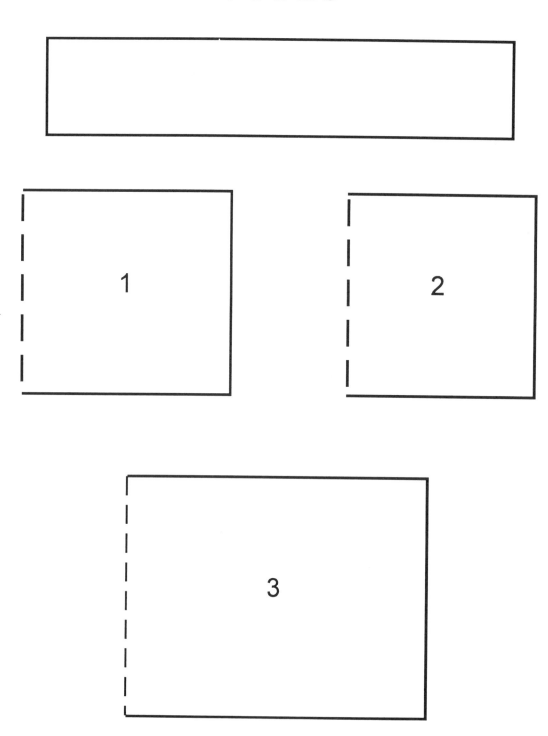

Jesus has power over _ _ _ _ _ _ _.

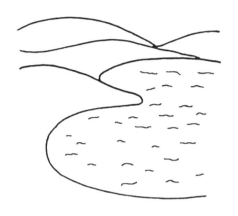

stills the storm
Mark 4:35-41

Jesus' disciples were frightened. They thought their boat would sink. They thought Jesus did not care if they died.

But Jesus **did** care. He commanded the storm to stop - and it did!

Jesus kept his disciples safe.

Can God keep me safe?

List some of the things and situations that make you afraid:

What should you do about them?

Preparation:
Read Mark 5:21-43, using the
Bible study notes to help you.

Lesson aim:
To teach that Jesus has power over death,
because he is God.

5:41   Again, Jesus speaks the word and it is done
(cf. previous miracles in this series).

5:43   Complete restoration is shown by the girl's
need for food.

Concentrate on the story of Jairus' daughter. You will
need to mention Mark 5:25-34 as the reason why
Jesus was held up, but do not go into great detail.

5:22   Jairus was an important man; it was his job
to supervise the synagogue services,
appoint who should read, who should pray
and who should preach. He showed his
recognition of Jesus' authority by falling at
his feet.

5:25-34   Jesus was in no hurry to go to Jairus' house.
God's timing is always right.

5:37   Peter, James and John were the 'inner
cabinet', the ones Jesus took with him on
special occasions. Later they were to
witness the transfiguration.

5:38   It was the custom for professional mourners
to come to the house and weep and wail
and make a noise.

5:39   Jesus also refers to death as sleep in John
11:11 (cf. 1 Thessalonians 4:13-14). The girl
was definitely dead - see the mourners'
reaction in Mark 5:40.

Lesson Plan

Start by seeing if the children remember the meaning
of authority (the power to enforce obedience). Ask
them who has authority over them and how that
authority is enforced. Recap on the previous 3 weeks'
lessons - what Jesus has authority over, how that
authority was demonstrated and what this teaches us
about Jesus. Revise the memory verse.

After the story stress the lesson aim. Go over what
response is required from the children. Death is a
difficult concept for young children. We need to major
on Jesus being in control and being with them at all
times, even sad ones.

Visual aids

Pictures or flannelgraph. You need Jesus, Peter,
James, John, Jairus, his wife, his daughter, a crowd,
some mourners (optional), a bed. Flannelgraph is
effective as the girl can 'get up'.

Activities / 3 - 5s

Photocopy page 67 for each child. Card or thick paper
gives a better result. Follow instructions on the page.

Activities / 5 - 7s

The children will make a clothes peg figure of Jairus'
daughter and her bed. You require a wooden clothes
peg and a pipe cleaner for each child, scraps of
material, 1 sponge cloth for every 6 children, rubber
bands and wool for hair. Before the lesson cut out a
face for each figure from pink paper using the template

on page 66. Also cut out a robe from material for each figure using the robe template. Cut the neck slit on each robe.

Activity time

1. Cover the top of the clothes peg with pink paper to make a face (see diagram).

2. Wrap a pipe cleaner round the peg below the pink paper to make arms. Colour the feet.

3. Place the robe over the head and secure round the waist with a rubber band.

4. Glue on strands of wool for hair and draw on a face.

5. To make the bed, cut a piece of sponge cloth approximately 10 x 5 cm for a mattress and a piece of material the same size for a cover. A cotton wool ball could be used for a pillow. Old tea towels are a good and inexpensive source of material for the bed covers. This makes a reasonably accurate representation of a first century bed. When not in use it would be rolled up and put away.

It is helpful if you make one beforehand to show the children.

Activities / 7 - 9s

The children continue with their activity books. Photocopy pages 68, 69, 70 (GNB & NIV) or 71 (KJV), and 72 for each child. Prior to the lesson prepare page 68 by cutting along the solid lines around the 4 windows so that the children can fold them back along the dotted lines. Glue page 69 behind page 68 so that the pictures are visible through the opened windows. Add the photocopied pages to the back of the activity books. The page of map symbols should be with the activity books.

Instructions

1. Use page 68 to review the previous 3 weeks' lessons and introduce this week's story. The children fill in 'forgive sin', 'disease', 'nature', 'death' and 'God' in the appropriate places.

2. Remind the children that in the previous lesson they discovered they need never be afraid. Use the story of Jairus' daughter to promote a discussion on 'what happens when I die?'
   The sort of questions to give some thought to are:
   - what happens when I/grandparents/parents/pets die?
   - why do we have to die?
   - do we go straight to heaven?
   - why do we bury/cremate the body? Will it hurt?
   - will I know people in heaven?
   - will my pets go to heaven?
   - is it wrong to be sad when someone I love/my pet dies?
   NB Death is the thing we are most afraid of. We all have to go through it. The one whom we trust (Jesus) has control over it, because **nothing** is outside his control.
   Remind them at the end that Jesus is always with them (Hebrews 13:5) - they do not need to be afraid.

3. Complete pages 70 or 71, and 72. The puzzle should be done as a class activity as this enables the less academically able to keep up with the others.

4. Cut out the appropriate symbol from page 45 and glue it to the map. Draw an arrow from the symbol to the place where the miracle happened.

5. Use the puzzle page to revise the memory verse.

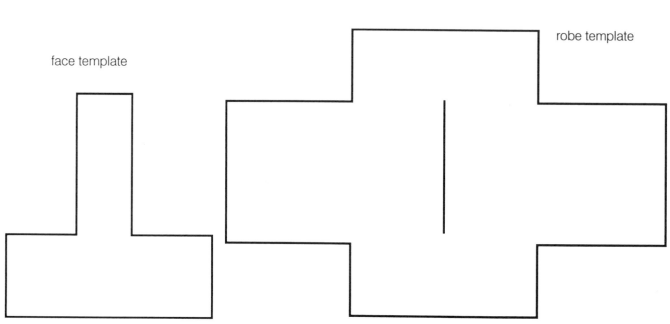

face template

robe template

Prior to the lesson cut off the strip at the top of this page and cut out the girl. Cut along the thick black line around the top of the bed clothes. The children colour the picture and the little girl. Attach the girl to the picture by slotting the tail end through the slit and securing with a split pin paper fastener at the 2 dots. The little girl can lie down and sit up when Jesus brings her back to life.

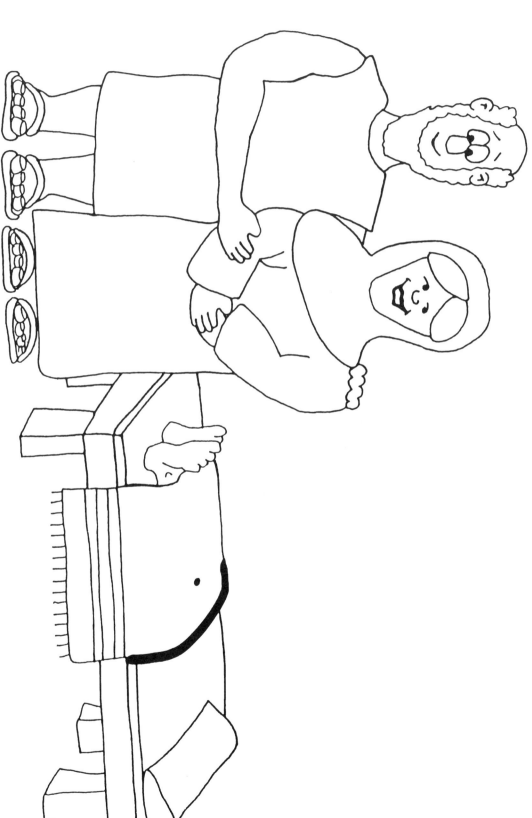

Jesus Christ is Lord. Philippians 2:11

Jesus has power

1	2
to _ _ _ _ _ _ _ _ _	over _ _ _ _ _ _ _
3	4
over _ _ _ _ _ _ _	over _ _ _ _ _ _

because he is _ _ _ _ .

Using the Bible to help you, answer the questions from the passage and place your answers in the grid below. The column indicated by the arrow will provide the missing word from your memory verse. The story is found in the book of Mark. The numbers in brackets tell you what chapter and verse to look up.

1. Jesus went to the other side of the .... (5:21)

2. Who asked Jesus to go with him? (5:22-23)

3. Which person in Jairus' family was ill? (5:23)

4. What did Jairus want Jesus to place on is daughter? (5:23)

5. Who else was ill? (5:25)

6. What did Jesus tell Jairus not to be? (5:36)

7. What did Jesus tell Jairus to do? (5:36)

8. The name of one of the disciples who went with Jesus. (5:37)

9. What did Jesus hear at Jairus' house? (5:38)

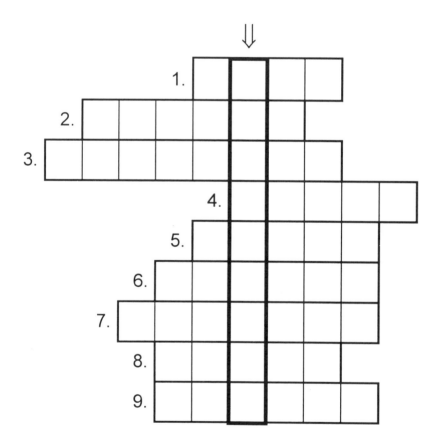

Jesus said, "I have been given all _ _ _ _ _ _ _ _ _ _
in heaven and on earth." *Matthew 28:18*

Because of this, Jesus was able to bring the little girl back to life.

Using the Bible to help you, answer the questions from the passage and place your answers in the grid below. The column indicated by the arrow will provide the missing word from your memory verse. The story is found in the book of Mark. The numbers in brackets tell you what chapter and verse to look up.

1. A ruler of the .... came to Jesus. (5:22)

2. The name of the man who asked Jesus to go with him? (5:22-23)

3. Which person in Jairus' family was ill? (5:23)

4. What did Jairus want Jesus to place on is daughter? (5:23)

5. Who else was ill? (5:25)

6. What did Jesus tell Jairus not to be? (5:36)

7. What did Jesus tell Jairus to do? (5:36)

8. The name of one of the disciples who went with Jesus. (5:37)

9. How quickly did the girl get better? (5:42)

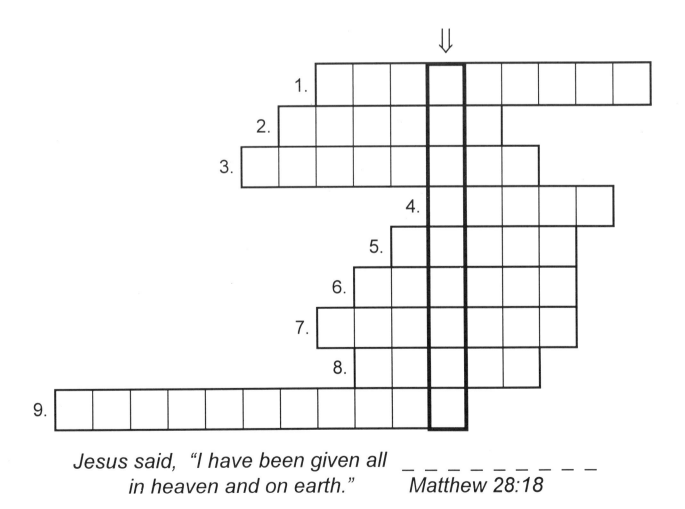

Jesus said, "I have been given all _ _ _ _ _ _ _ _ _
in heaven and on earth."   *Matthew 28:18*

Because of this, Jesus was able to bring the little girl back to life.

Jesus has power over

I need never be afraid, because he has promised he will never leave me. (Hebrews 13:5)

Cut off the bottom strip and cut out the girl.
Using a split pin paper fastener, attach the girl to the bed at the dots.
The girl can be swivelled from a lying to a standing position.

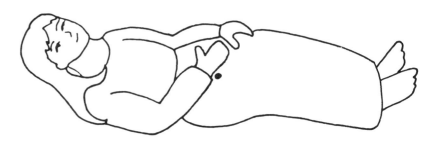

Preparation:
Read Luke 8:26-39, using the Bible study notes to help you.

Lesson aim:
To teach that Jesus has power over demons, because he is God.

In the Bible there are very few references to demon-possession outside the gospels. It appears to be a phenomenon especially associated with the earthly ministry of Jesus and should probably be interpreted as an outburst of demoniacal opposition to the work of Jesus. Ordinary human beings do not have authority over demons and even Jesus' opponents recognised his ability to do this and that this power was not human (although they attributed it to the indwelling of Satan, Luke 11:14-20).

The gospel records show that Jesus distinguished between ordinary illness and that associated with demon possession (Matthew 10:8, Mark 6:13). The former were treated by laying on of hands or anointing (e.g. Mark 1:30-31; 1:41), the latter by commanding the demon to depart (e.g. Mark 1:25-26).

8:26   The city of Gerasa was 30 miles south-east of the lake, but it is thought that its territory probably extended to the lakeside. Gergesa (on the shore of the lake) is thought to be the actual site of the incident.

8:31   The abyss was the abode of the demons (Revelation 9:1-11).

8:32   Pork was forbidden food for the Jews, but the eastern side of Lake Galilee was largely non Jewish.

Lesson Plan

Demon possession is outside the experience of the majority of children of this age group. In this story it should be explained as the man having lots of evil spirits living in him which made him behave in a

strange way (detail his behaviour). The evil spirits also made him very strong and people were very frightened of him.

Start the lesson by recapping on the previous lessons of the series. Photocopy pages 68 and 69 at A3 size as a visual aid. For instructions regarding their use, see page 66, activity for 7-9s. Use the picture of the crown at the top of page 68 to lead into the meaning of 'authority'. Revise the memory verse. In today's true story from the Bible we will find out about something else Jesus has power over.

At the end of the story stress the change in the man after Jesus healed him - able to sit still, clothed, in his right mind. Finish by pointing out that Jesus is more powerful than Satan because he is God.

Visual aids

Draw a background scene of hillside and lake on a large sheet of paper (A1 or A2). Make 2 slits (see diagram on page 74). Make a drawing of pigs on a long strip of paper. The paper must be long enough to pass through the background without coming out (see diagram). Thread 'pigs' strip through the slits. (NB background on 'pigs' strip must match up with the background of the picture.)

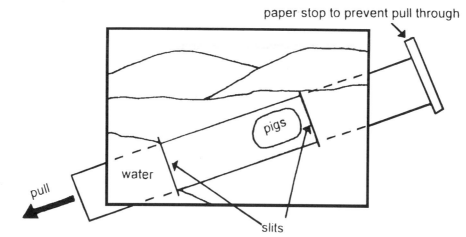

paper stop to prevent pull through

pigs

water

pull

slits

This background can be used minus the 'pigs' strip to tell other Bible stories, so is worth preserving. Cover the background with clear plastic adhesive as this allows the figures to be moved on and off without damaging it.

Pictures - the man whilst demon possessed, the man in his right mind, swineherd, Jesus, disciples, crowd of people. Stick the figures onto the background with bluetak.

When the time comes for the pigs to be drowned, pull the "pigs" strip so that the pigs race into the lake. (Sellotape on the edge of the lake slit facilitates passage of the paper strip.

Activities / 3 - 5s

Photocopy pages 75 and 76 for each child, preferably on card. Prior to the lesson cut out pigs, the demoniac arc from page 75 and the marked area on page 76. Cut along the dotted line on page 76 to make a slit.

Instructions
1. The children colour the 2 pictures of the demoniac on the arc, the pigs and the picture.
2. Attach the demoniac arc behind the picture using a split pin paper fastener through the dots on the arc and above the cut out area. Make sure the arc will rotate behind the picture.
3. Put the tail of the pigs cut-out through the slit on page 76 and attach it to the back of the picture using a split pin paper fastener through the dots.
4. Start with the demoniac in chains visible in the cut out section of the picture (a tomb) and the pigs on dry land. As Jesus heals the demoniac swivel the pigs through the slit in the picture into the water and rotate the demoniac arc to show him seated and in is right mind.

Activities / 5 - 7s

Each child requires page 77 photocopied on card and a sheet of A4 plain paper.
Instructions
1. Cut off the strip containing the figures from page 77.
2. Colour the figures.
3. Colour the rest of the page as follows:
   land - green, cliff - grey/brown, sea - blue.

4. Fold the coloured page and glue to the sheet of plain paper (see diagrams).

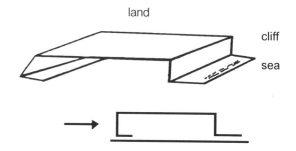

land

cliff

sea

5. Cut out the figures, fold the tabs under and glue them onto the scenery where appropriate.

Activities / 7 - 9s

The children continue with their activity books. These, together with the page of map symbols (page 45), should be in the class basket at Sunday school. Photocopy pages 78 and 79 for each child and add to the back of the activity book.
Instructions
1. At the start of the lesson review the previous 4 weeks - Jesus came as king and demonstrated his power to forgive sin, over disease, nature and death. Remind them that they learned that Jesus is always with them; nothing, not even death, can separate them from him. Use page 78 to introduce the topic for today - Jesus even has power over demons.
2. Tell the story. At the end stress the difference in the man after Jesus had healed him - sitting, clothed, in his right mind. Possible questions to use with the group:
   - As a result of being healed, was the man more or less able to relate to other people?
   - Does knowing Jesus affect the way we relate to people? In what way does it make a difference?
   - Why were the people of Gerasa so afraid?
   It is unlikely that this age group will bring up much about demons, demon possession, etc.
3. Complete page 79.
4. Cut out the appropriate symbol from page 45 and glue onto the map. Draw an arrow from the symbol to where the miracle took place.
5. Revise the memory verse.

Philippians 2:11

Jesus Christ is Lord.

cut out

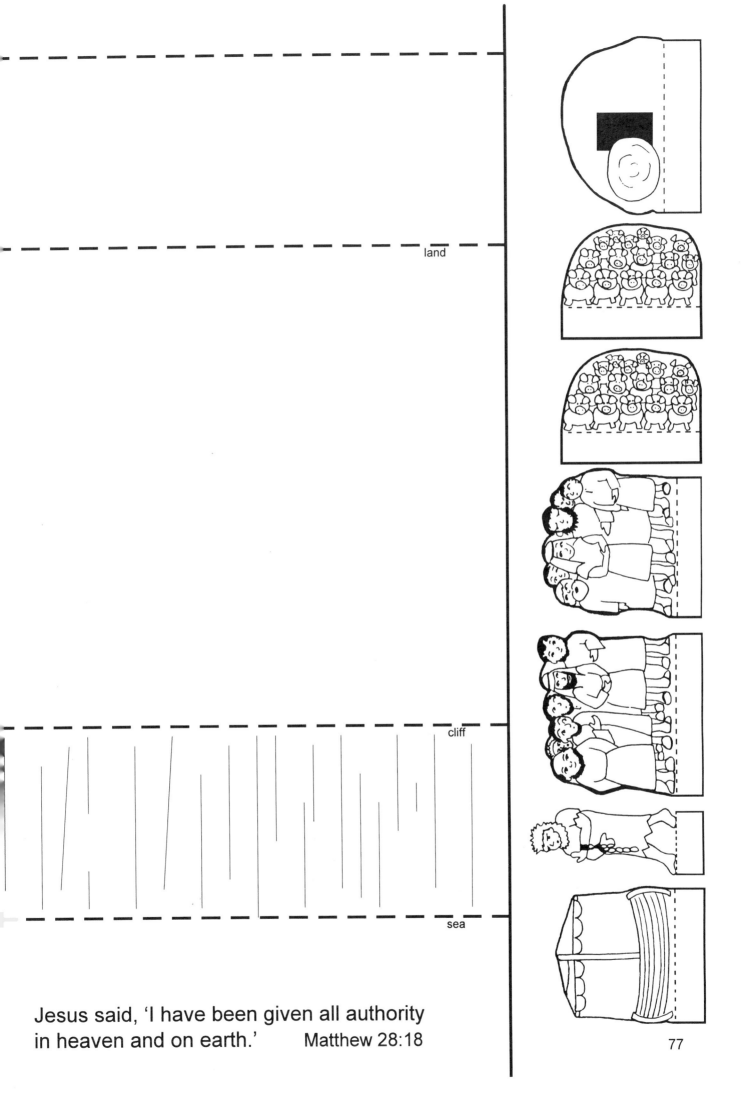

land

cliff

sea

Jesus said, 'I have been given all authority
in heaven and on earth.'   Matthew 28:18

Use this key to decode the Bible verse written below.

✎	●	✉	🚂	🛋	🧸	🪟	👫	🚿	🪜	⛵	🚃	🌐
a	b	c	d	e	f	g	h	i	j	k	l	m

🎁	🎣	🌧	☁	🌨	☁	☀	☁	🌞	🧳	⚽	✒	🚲
n	o	p	q	r	s	t	u	v	w	x	y	z

_ _ _ _ _ _ _   can separate us from   _ _ _ ' _   love:

neither   _ _ _ _ _ _   nor   _ _ _ _ ,   neither   _ _ _ _ _ _   nor

other heavenly   _ _ _ _ _ _ _   or   _ _ _ _ _ _ _ ,   neither the

_ _ _ _ _ _ _ _   nor the   _ _ _ _ _ _ ,   neither the   _ _ _ _ _

_ _ _ _ _   nor the   _ _ _ _ _   _ _ _ _ _   - there is

_ _ _ _ _ _ _   in all   _ _ _ _ _ _ _ _   that will ever be able

to   _ _ _ _ _ _ _ _ _   us from the   _ _ _ _ _ _ _ _ _

which is ours through   _ _ _ _ _ _   _ _ _ _ _   our   _ _ _ _ .

Romans 8:36-39 (GNB)

78

Jesus' Authority Over Demons

Luke 8:26-39

Draw a picture of the man before and after Jesus healed him.

before   after

What was different about him after Jesus had healed him?

Jesus has power over _ _ _ _ _ _

because he is _ _ _ .

Preparation:
Read Mark 6:30-44, using the Bible study notes to help you.

Lesson aim:
To teach that Jesus has power to provide what is needful, because he is God.

6:30   This is the only time that Mark refers to the disciples as 'apostles'. This term refers to their job as 'messengers' (Mark 6:6-13).

6:33,44 It is difficult for small children to understand how many people were involved. To give them some idea take a building they all know and ask them to imagine it packed full of people standing up - it would be even more people than that (twice as many, etc. depending on the size of the building).

6:35-38 Jesus was concerned for people's physical needs as well as for their spiritual ones.

6:37   200 silver coins was the equivalent of about 8 months' wages.

6:38   The bread would have been a kind of cake made from barley, the size of a dinner plate and about 2 cm thick.

6:41   The phrase 'he gave them' implies (in the Greek) that it was Jesus who was actually multiplying the bread and constantly giving the disciples further supplies to hand round.

Lesson Plan

Start by revising the previous 5 lessons. Jesus came as king and demonstrated his power in remarkable ways - forgiving sin, healing disease, controlling the forces of nature, raising from the dead, banishing demons. Revise the memory verse. Is this powerful king only concerned about the big things, or can we be confident that he cares about the little things like our daily food?

After the story point out to the children that we can be confident that Jesus does care about the little things. Talk with the children about the things they need every day and the importance of asking God for them, recognising that they come from God. You will need to discuss how God provides for our needs, e.g. through parents earning money to pay for our food and clothes, sun and rain to allow the food to grow, etc. Finish by having a time of prayer, thanking God for his provision. Encourage the children to pray simple prayers, e.g. 'Dear Lord Jesus, thank you for my food. Amen.'

Visual aids

A basket containing 5 bread rolls and 2 cardboard fish. Cover the fish with kitchen foil to give a shiny appearance. When you get to the part where the bread is broken, break the rolls and hand a piece to each child.

You also need 12 individual pictures of a basket to stick up on the board one by one to show how much was left over. For 5s and older, one word of the memory verse can be written on each basket, with the reference on the twelfth basket (see page 85). These can then be used to revise the memory verse.

Activities / 3 - 5s

Photocopy page 82 on card for every 4 children. Each child requires 2 fish, 5 cotton wool balls, a paper plate, glue and glitter. The children put glue on each fish and shake on glitter. To do this without making too much mess place the fish in the bottom of an ice cream container or box before shaking on the glitter. Alternatively the fish can be coloured. Glue the fish onto the paper plate and add the 5 cotton wool balls for 'loaves'. Ask each child to recite the memory verse and write it on the rim of the plate when they answer. For a large class the memory verse can be written on the rim of the plates before the lesson.

Activities / 5 - 7s

Fish and Bread Lotto. Each child requires a paper plate and page 83 photocopied on card. Prior to the lesson cut out a set of fish and loaves and place in an envelope for each child. Prepare the paper plates by writing 7 answers on each plate (see the questions below). Make sure that each plate has a different combination of answers. Write out the questions and answers on individual strips of paper (or on loaves and fish) and place in a container.

Give each child a paper plate and a set of fish and loaves. Pull out a question from the box and ask it. Each child who has the answer written on their plate covers it with a fish or a loaf. The winner is the first child to cover all 7 answers. Plates can be mixed up and reallocated and the game repeated. Younger children may need help with reading the answers.

Questions

1. Jesus wanted to take his disciples to a lonely what?   *place*

2. How did they get there?   *boat*

3. Jesus had pity on the crowd because they were like sheep without a what?   *shepherd*

4. Jesus taught the crowd what?   *many things*

5. After Jesus had taught them the crowd became very what?   *hungry*

6. When it became late what did the disciples ask Jesus to do?   *send the crowd away*

7. Who did Jesus say should give the crowd something to eat?   *the disciples*

8. How much would it have cost to feed everyone? *8 months' wages*

9. How many loaves did the boy have?   *5*

10. How many fish did the boy have?   *2*

11. How many men were present?   *5,000*

12. How many people sat down in each group? *50 - 100*

13. Where did the people sit down?   *the grass*

14. Jesus could do this miracle because he is who? *God*

Activities / 7 - 9s

The children continue with their activity books. These should be in the class baskets at Sunday school, together with the sheets of map symbols (page 45). Each child requires pages 84 and 85 photocopied and an A4 sheet of plain paper. Add page 84 and the plain sheet of paper to the back of the activity books.

Instructions

Prior to the lesson give some thought to the following questions:

- Should we worry about daily needs? (Remind them of the Lord's prayer)
- Does this mean I don't need to do anything to provide for myself?
- What is the difference between 'needs' and 'desires'?
- Does God give me whatever I want?

1. Review the previous 5 weeks' lessons - Jesus came as king and demonstrated his power to forgive sin, over disease, nature, death and demons.

2. Tell the story.

3. Complete the puzzle on page 84. Fill in the Bible verse in the spaces provided inside the circle. Fill in the missing numbers - 5, 2, 5,000. Then fill in 'provide' and 'God' in the spaces in the sentence below. Discuss the 2 questions at the bottom of the page.

4. Cut out the appropriate symbol from page 45 and glue to the map. Draw an arrow from the symbol to where the miracle took place.

5. At the top of the plain sheet of paper write 'Jesus said,'. Cut out the shapes from page 85. Glue the 5 loaves in the top right hand corner of the plain page. Glue the 12 baskets and 2 fish onto the page in the correct order to give the memory verse.

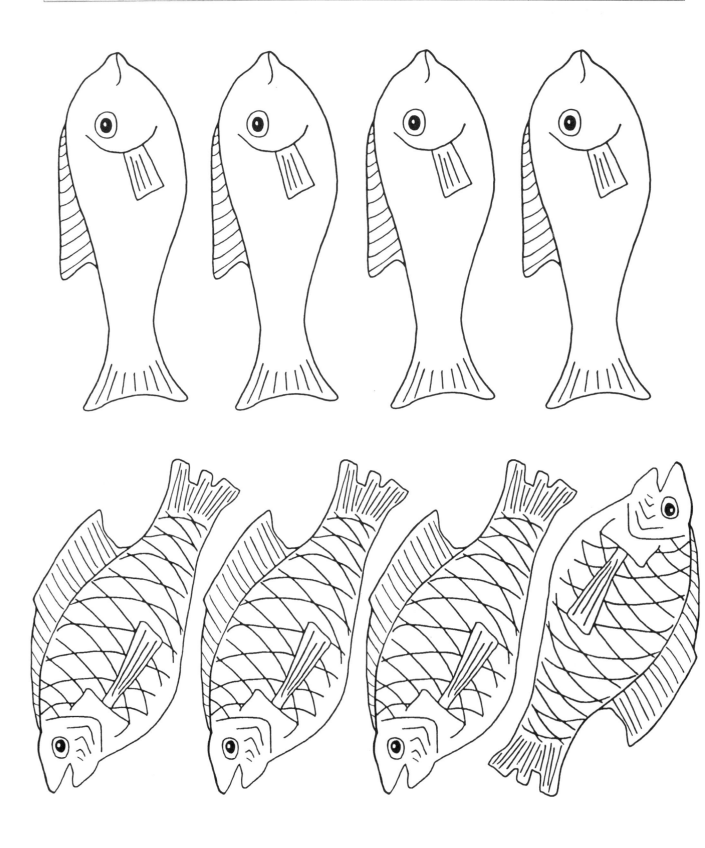

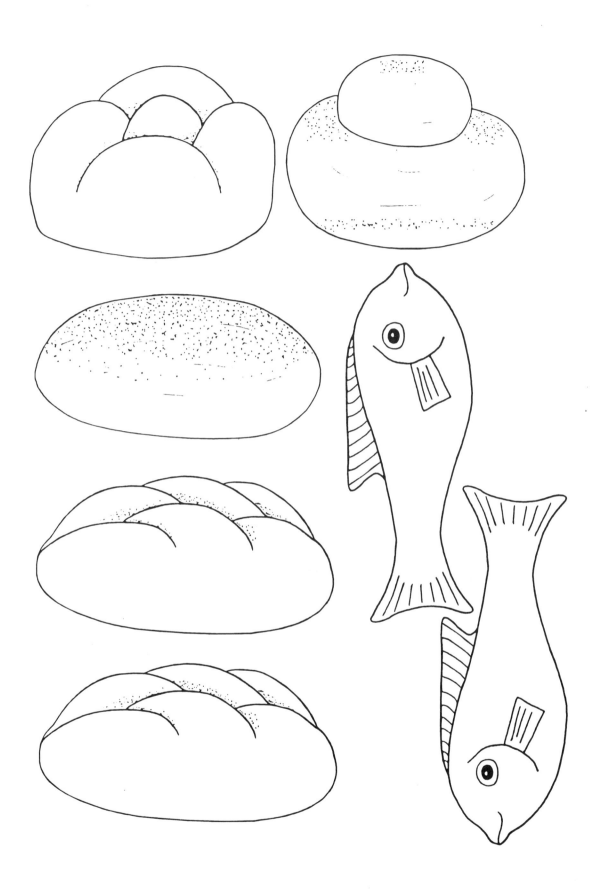

Start at the arrow and write down every third letter in the spaces provided inside the circle to discover what God has promised.

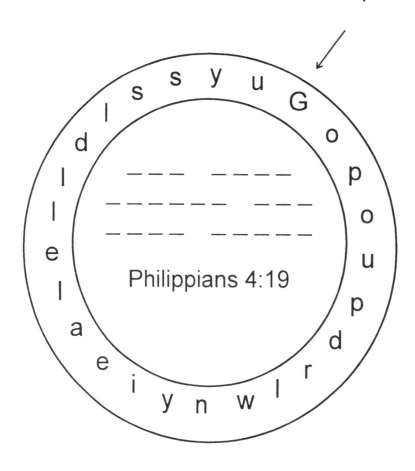

Philippians 4:19

Jesus used .... loaves and .... fish to feed .... men, as well as women and children.

Jesus has power to _ _ _ _ _ _ _ because he is _ _ _.

Discuss

What does this mean for me?

Will God give me whatever I ask for?

all

been

Matthew

given

heaven

28

authority

have

in

on

and

earth

18

I

Preparation:
Read Luke 19:1-10, using the Bible study notes to help you.

Lesson aim:
To teach that Jesus has power to save men, because he is God.

19:2   As chief tax-collector Zacchaeus was responsible for the collection of taxes over a wide area. There would have been sub-collectors under his control.

19:4   Sycamores were evergreen, fig-bearing trees, 20-30 feet tall, with short trunks and widely spreading branches.

19:7   Strict Jews regarded tax collectors, because of their continual contact with Gentiles, as ceremonially unclean, so would not eat with them.

19:8   Note the change in Zacchaeus. 'Four times the amount' was far more than that required by the law (Leviticus 6:4-5).

The children need to understand that God's salvation is for everyone, good and bad, and that salvation results in a changed life. Obviously, the way you present this will need to be carefully thought out with regard to the age group you are teaching.

Lesson Plan

This is the last lesson of the series. Photocopy page 90 at A3, colour the symbols representing the previous 6 lessons, cut them out and mount on card or paper. Use these to review what we have learnt about Jesus in the series so far. Remind the children that this powerful God loves us and cares for us, even in the small things. Talk about the response God requires from us - trust and obedience. The problem is, however hard we try, we still disobey and do wrong things. Is Jesus powerful enough to change us and make us fit for heaven?

At the end of the story point out the change in Zacchaeus. Talk about our need to say sorry to Jesus and to ask for forgiveness. Remind the children of Jesus' ability to forgive sin (lesson 1 of the series). Revise the memory verse.

Visual aids

Flannelgraph or pictures or stand up figures.

For stand up figures glue the figures onto card with a flat base and back support (see diagram).

Figures required are Jesus, disciples, Zacchaeus, and a crowd. Make sure Zacchaeus is shorter than other men. For stand up figures you need a tree with a platform at the back for Zacchaeus to stand on.

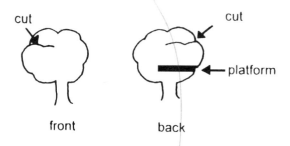

front   back

Activities / 3 - 5s

Each child requires:
- a cardboard tube from a toilet roll or paper towel,
- 2 treetops cut from green card (see templates on page 88),
- 2 feet, 2 hands and 1 head cut from pink gummed paper.

Activity time

1. Glue the tree tops to the cardboard tube as shown. Glue the tree tops together at the top.

2. Draw a face and hair on the cut-out head and glue it to one side of the tree top. Stick the hands on the same side as the head and the feet on the other side (see diagram).

Activities / 5 - 7s

The children will make a model of Zacchaeus up his tree. Each child requires page 89 photocopied on card and an A4 sheet of green paper. Prior to the lesson cut out the figure of Zacchaeus, the tree trunk and the square with the memory verse written on it.

Activity time

1. The children colour the tree trunk brown. Help them to roll it into a tube and glue.

2. Roll the sheet of green paper into a tube lengthways. Insert this through the middle of the tree trunk so that about 1½ cm protrudes from the bottom. Cut 4 slits in the bottom protrusion and multiple slits in the top for branches.

3. Splay out the bottom 4 sections of the green paper and glue to the middle of the square base sheet. Splay open the top section to make branches.

4. Colour Zacchaeus and fold him in half. Glue his hands and feet to the tree. The feet are glued either side of the tree trunk and the hands to branches.

Do remind the children that Zacchaeus climbed up a sycamore tree as this tree looks more like a palm tree!

Activities / 7 - 9s

The children complete their activity books today. The books, together with the page containing the remaining map symbol, should be in the class baskets at Sunday school. Photocopy pages 90 and 91 for each child and add to the back of the activity books. Each child also requires 2 garden sticks or lengths of dowel approximately 25 cm long and a length of wool to make a hanging loop.

Instructions

1. Review the previous 6 lessons using page 90 - Jesus came as king and demonstrated his power to forgive sin, over disease, nature, death and demons, and to provide for our needs. The children fill in 'forgive sin', 'disease', 'nature', 'death', 'demons' and 'provide' (going clockwise). Fill in 'God' at the bottom.

2. Tell the story.

3. Fill in 'change men' on page 90. Discuss with the children that Jesus has power to change **all** men, even them, to make them more Christ-like. Prior to the lesson give some thought to what this means in daily life for a 7-9 year old.

4. As this is the last lesson of the series make sure you tie it all together. The Lord Jesus, whom we worship, demonstrated that he is God and king. Our response should be acknowledgement of who he is and obedience to his word (John 14:15). Do make sure that the children realise that the salvation God offers is a free gift (point back to the Christmas series) and cannot be earned by good deeds.

5. Cut out the remaining symbol from page 45 and glue to the map. Draw an arrow from the symbol to where the miracle took place.

6. Use page 91 to make a wall hanging. Colour the page and glue the top and bottom round a stick. Make a hanging loop at the top.

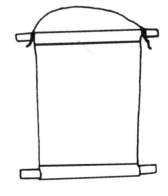

The books can be taken home.

Templates for model of Zacchaeus up a tree.

tree top template

cut 2

hands

heaven and on earth.'

Matthew 28:18

given all authority in

Jesus said, 'I have been

Jesus has

to _ _ _ _ _ _ _ _ _ _

to _ _ _ _ _ _ _ _ _ _

over _ _ _ _ _ _ _ _

to _ _ _ _ _ _ _

power

over _ _ _ _ _ _

over _ _ _ _ _

over _ _ _ _ _ _

because he is _ _ _.

My Prayer

Thank you,

Lord Jesus, that you are

King of all creation, and

nothing is outside your control.

Please help me to be

obedient to your

Word.

Amen

Syllabus for On the Way for 3-9s

	Year 1	Year 2	Year 3
	Book 1 (13 weeks)	**Book 6 (10 weeks)**	**Book 11 (13 weeks)**
Old/New Testament	In the Beginning (3) Abraham (6) Jacob (4)	Samson (2) Ruth (2) Samuel (2) Saul (4)	Jesus Meets (3) God's Rules (10)
	Book 2 (12 weeks)	**Book 7 (13 weeks)**	**Book 12 (14 weeks)**
Christmas *New Testament*	Christmas Gifts (5) Jesus' Authority (7)	The Christmas Story (4) Preparation for Service (4) The Promised Messiah (5)	Heavenly Messengers (5) Jesus Helps (5) Parables of the Kingdom (4)
	Book 3 (13 weeks)	**Book 8 (9 weeks)**	**Book 13 (13 weeks)**
New Testament *Easter* *Early Church*	Prayer (4) Jesus is King (5) Peter (4)	Jesus Teaches (5) Parables of Judgment (2) The Easter Story (2)	Parables of the Vineyard (3) Jesus our Redeemer (3) The Early Church (3) Paul (4)
	Book 4 (10 weeks)	**Book 9 (10 weeks)**	**Book 14 (14 weeks)**
Old Testament	Joseph (4) Job (1) Moses (5)	David (7) Solomon (3)	Kings (5) Daniel (4) Esther (2) Nehemiah (3)
	Book 5 (10 weeks)	**Book 10 (11 weeks)**	
Old Testament	In the Wilderness (4) Joshua (4) Gideon (2)	Elijah (5) Elisha (4) Jonah (2)	

The books can be used in any order; the above plan is the suggested order.
The syllabus is chronological; Christmas to Easter is all about Jesus, followed by 3 series on the early church (1 in Book 3 and 2 in Book 13). The rest of each year consists of lessons from the Old Testament. Old Testament and New Testament lessons are in separate books (apart from Book 11), so the books can be used in whatever order is required. The books contain differing numbers of lessons, so that they fit the required number of weeks between Christmas and Easter and the following Christmas. The number in brackets indicates the number of lessons in a series.

For more information about *On The Way for 3-9s* please contact:
Christian Focus Publications, Geanies House, Fearn, Tain, Ross shire, IV20 1TW / Tel: (01862) 871 541 or TnT Ministries, 29 Buxton Gardens, Acton, London, W3 9LE / Tel: (0181) 992 0450

Teacher's Challenge Solution

 pages 17, 24, 29, 57, 73 and 86.